SELECTED POEMS

ELIZABETH BARRETT BROWNING was born in 1806 into a prosperous family. She grew up at the family home near Hereford, until the family moved to London in 1838. She was well educated at home, and her abilities were encouraged by her protective and authoritarian father, who paid for the first publication of her poetry when she was fourteen. From an early age she suffered from ill health, aggravated by an injury to her spine, and she lived a confined life as an invalid, though she became a well-known and admired poet. A correspondence with Robert Browning, who had written to her after the publication of her *Poems* of 1844, led to their secret marriage and elopement to Italy in 1846. Elizabeth Barrett Browning lived for the rest of her life in the Casa Guidi in Florence, where she found a new personal freedom and witnessed the struggle for Italian independence from Austrian control. She died in Florence in 1861.

MALCOLM HICKS is a senior lecturer in the Department of English and American Studies at the University of Manchester. His publications include the *Selected Poems* of Aphra Behn for the Fyfield series, for which he has also edited the *Selected Poems* of Oscar Wilde.

D1542742

Fyfield*Books* aim to make available some of the great classics of British and European literature in clear, affordable formats, and to restore often neglected writers to their place in literary tradition.

Fyfield*Books* take their name from the Fyfield elm in Matthew Arnold's 'Scholar Gypsy' and 'Thyrsis'. The tree stood not far from the village where the series was originally devised in 1971.

> *Roam on! The light we sought is shining still.*
> *Dost thou ask proof? Our tree yet crowns the hill,*
> *Our Scholar travels yet the loved hill-side*

from 'Thyrsis'

ELIZABETH BARRETT BROWNING

Selected Poems

Edited with an introduction by
MALCOLM HICKS

FyfieldBooks

CARCANET

First published in Great Britain in 1983 by
Carcanet Press Limited
Alliance House
Cross Street
Manchester M2 7AQ

This impression 2003

Selection, introduction and editorial matter
© Malcolm Hicks 1983, 1988, 2003

A CIP catalogue record for this book is available from the British Library
ISBN 1 85754 700 4

The publisher acknowledges financial assistance from
the Arts Council of England

Printed and bound in England by SRP Ltd, Exeter

CONTENTS

INTRODUCTION

The progress of Elizabeth Barrett Browning's reputation is surely unique in English literary history. A poetic career which constantly overshadowed that of her now much more celebrated husband has itself been eclipsed by the popular after-fame of her romance and elopement drawn from the almost too well rehearsed details of her private life. In an insidiously patronizing way which would have incensed the ardently feminist Mrs. Browning, the world has delighted to find that an extremely—not to say excessively—learned 'poetess' turns out not to be a blue-stocking after all; and since the death in 1861 of the writer who was seriously considered as first woman Poet Laureate to succeed Wordsworth (actually, Tennyson got the job), a stream of biographies and collections of letters has emerged which shows no signs of abating. The creative achievement, however, which alone would justify such an intense involvement, has been allowed to languish to the extent that, significantly, apart from fugitive reappearances of the love poems covertly addressed to Robert Browning, the *Sonnets from the Portuguese*, the recent republication of the feminist poetic novel, *Aurora Leigh*, and a scholarly edition of *Casa Guidi Windows*, no collection of her poetry has materialized for half a century. In our age of specialization, it is all too common to find some one or other partisan insisting that his or her favourite deserves more than localized notice in the scholarly magazines, but it would be wrong to think of Elizabeth Barrett Browning as belonging to this class. Yet, for aesthetic reasons as much as economic ones, the murmuring among professionals for a complete edition of her work is equally extravagant: she is an uneven writer who gradually won through to poetic maturity; and if served by a best, yet still to some extent representative, selection— as this purports to be—much will have been done to rectify the balance of interest.

Born in 1806 into a prosperous family where her talents were readily encouraged, Elizabeth Barrett virtually lisped in numbers.

With an eager and general absorption in the Classics, and a felt sense of the progress of poetry from the age of Pope and beyond to the Romantic groundswell of these her early years, she inherited an ambitious sense of the poet's calling. She earnestly appreciated the traditional public role of poetry to teach, but she also read her Neoplatonists, her Longinus, and enthusiastically supported the emphasis upon individual inspiration as a means of intuiting universal, even mystical, truths, which had been gathering momentum among both practitioners and theorists during the course of the eighteenth century. But at this early stage, the self-conscious assertiveness and precocity of the prefaces to the *Battle of Marathon* (1820) and the encyclopaedic *Essay on Mind* (1826) are tempered by the fact that, in the verse itself, the eager apprentice is sensibly content to exercise her impressive powers of imitation. The manner of Pope is a sufficient curb on both form and content; yet, rightly, this could not be expected to last. With an ardour heightened by her invalidism (her first serious incapacity had occurred after the completion of *Marathon*), and (not to be too cynical) a subtle exploitation of her more generalized weakness as a female, she was determined to number in the male pantheon. Inspired by a fervour at least the equal of Shelley's, Byron's, and their 'Spasmodic' followers, she for her part endeavoured to reconcile a sentimental, domestic bias with a sublime overreaching into the infinite, and—to adapt Robert Browning's maxim—her reach much exceeded her grasp. At least until the *Poems* of 1844 her high aims dissolve into what the 'average' reader would instantly dismiss as gush: often religiose, lachrymose, and permeated with an overwrought, generalized mood of the autobiographical. Or we discover fantastic endeavours like the *Seraphim* of 1838, with its straining to present a divine perspective on the 'Crucifixion . . . the Angels of Heaven hav[ing] departed towards the Earth, except the two Seraphim, Ador the Strong and Zerah the Bright One. *The place [being] the outer side of the shut Heavenly Gate.*' Something of both the burden and exhilaration of high office can be detected in the following description of the poet from

8

Earth and her Praisers from the same volume:

> He, a poet! know him by
> The ecstasy-dilated eye,
> Not uncharged with tears that ran
> Upward from his heart of man;
> By the cheek, from hour to hour,
> Kindled bright or sunken wan
> With a sense of lonely power;
> By the brow uplifted higher
> Than others, for more low declining;
> By the lip which words of fire
> Overboiling have burned white
> While they gave the nations light:
> Ay, in every time and place
> Ye may know the poet's face
>   By the shade or shining.
>
> 'Neath a golden cloud he stands,
> Spreading his impassioned hands.
> 'O God's Earth!' he saith, 'the sign
> From the Father-soul to mine
> Of all beauteous mysteries,
> Or all perfect images
> Which, divine in His divine,
> In my human only are
> Very excellent and fair! . . .

Scenes and situations, which from a less quixotic temperament we would not hesitate to call arbitrary, are evoked for the sake of rapt poeticizing: 'Methought that I did stand upon a tomb— . . .'; 'I had a dream!—my spirit was unbound . . .'; and so on, which it would be tedious to rehearse any further. Yet from discussions in her letters to her earliest mentor, Hugh Stuart Boyd, and to her friend Miss Mitford; from the reaching at authoritative discrimination in the erudite prose reviews of the Greek Christian and English poets for the *Athenaeum* magazine (1844), we can determine a serious sense of criticism working alongside her practice of the divine craft, which begins to bear fruit in the *Poems* of 1844. As if sensing her own inability to sustain any constructive flight into the empyrean, we find her progressively inclined to refine upon her domestic intelligence, with a comparable easing in both technique and expression. It is aesthetically satisfying to find that the Miss Barrett who, despite the public disaster of *Sordello* (1840), was astute enough to persist in her belief in Robert Browning's promise, should draw from her impetuous fellow poet the unreserved praise which initiated an informed and informing friendship that led to love and marriage. 'I love your verse with all my heart, dear Miss Barrett', he wrote, a resounding echo of the general acclaim the 1844 volume enjoyed. It is not to the passions alone, however, that this collection fitfully makes its appeal. Not only the poet who was beginning to emerge from the shadow of Shelley to his first great monologues, but also the Tennyson of the *Princess* (first published 1847), who was to write *Maud* not long after, would relish the way in which, say, the essentially romantic narrative of *Lady Geraldine's Courtship* is spiced with compact social observation:

> And they praised me in her presence—'Will
> your book appear this summer?'
> Then returning to each other—'Yes, our
> plans are for the moors.'
> Then with whisper dropped behind me—
> 'There he is! the latest comer.
> Oh, she only likes his verses! what is over,
> she endures.'

Her more rarefied metaphysics are exchanged for the singular experiences of childhood, convincingly evoked in poems like the *Lost Bower* and *Romance of the Swan's Nest*; her vigorous passion for learning, engagingly modulated by her affection for the man with

whom she shared it, H. S. Boyd, ably registered in the *Wine of Cyprus*;
while the monologue, *Catarina to Camoens*—one of Browning's
favourites—is nicely judged with its bitter-sweet refrain echoing the
Portuguese poet's compliment to his forlorn mistress, '(Dying in his
absence abroad, and referring to the poem in which he recorded the
sweetness of her eyes)':

> When the palace-ladies, sitting
>> Round your gittern, shall have said,
>> 'Poet, sing those verses written
>> For the lady who is dead,'
>>> Will you tremble
>>> Yet dissemble,—
> Or sing hoarse, with tears between,
> 'Sweetest eyes were ever seen'?

How well, here, Elizabeth exploits her womanly instincts: a firm
talent she was to refine upon as she developed a profound, yet in-
cisive, ability to scrutinize sexual relationships.

It is tempting to relate this continuing refinement of her overly
'poetic' temperament to the fact that from the mid 1840s onward she
began an exchange of views with, and became the wife and constant
companion of, the man whose next substantial collection was to be
the *Men and Women* volume of 1854. There is, of course, more to the
story. She had wrested herself from excesses born of a life of confine-
ment to achieve success in an essentially male world. She had de-
veloped an acute independence of spirit as she painfully examined
the nature of her secret and protracted courtship in the household
of an emotionally tyrannical paterfamilias; and, following marriage
and elopement, she gained in knowledge and experience from living
in Italy and occasionally elsewhere on the Continent which helped
her to acquire a fine, frank sense of the way in which social, political,
and economic contexts inform the conduct of sexual passion. Here
at last was her sense of duty satisfied; here she might 'teach' without
strain. Self-elected torchbearer of grandiose notions of individual

poetic inspiration, her enthusiasm for learning and imitation had been a contributory factor in her equally insistent conservatism. For as heir to Classical, Renaissance, and Neo-Classical precepts she endorsed the idea that poets should never forget their obligations to instruct. What passed for universal insights, however, had been made to rest precariously upon private vision. Not least did force of circumstance come to the aid of her anxious self-criticisms at not being able to achieve a satisfying poetic unity: insights were becoming increasingly pragmatic and demanded their own chastened language. The earlier frenzy and ardour was being translated more and more into a precision of expression and pungency of tone which was to remain with her right through to the political protest poems with which her career was brought to a close. Eccentric Romantic yearnings had given way to a Victorian energy of mind faithful to the dictum of mixing profit with pleasure, and engaged upon perennially interesting subject matter.

Yet for all this the *Poems* of 1850 represent less of a consolidation of the merits found in the volume published six years earlier than one would have liked. The sonnet *The Prospect*, for example, apart from a trace of characteristic archaism, shows how a unique simile is betrayed in the elaboration:

> Methinks we do as fretful children do,
> Leaning their faces on the window-pane
> To sigh the glass dim with their own breath's stain,
> And shut the sky and landscape from their view:
> And thus, alas, since God the maker drew
> A mystic separation 'twixt those twain,—
> The life beyond us, and our souls in pain,—
> We miss the prospect which we are called unto
> By grief we are fools to use. Be still and strong,
> O man, my brother! Hold thy sobbing breath,
> And keep thy soul's large window pure from wrong!
> That so, as life's appointment issueth,

Thy vision may be clear to watch along
The sunset consummation-lights of death.

But in this mid-period it is greatly satisfying to look to the wealth of material the letters provide for the kind of intelligence and sensibility that was to nourish the best of the later poetry. Indeed, the following shrewd appraisal which she sent to Miss Mitford (Feb. 1845) shows how her 'breakthrough' was achieved against social and sexual odds quite outside her own control:

What I was going to say of men, or rather of a man,—was just this of Mr. Hunter. It might be amusing if it were not so vexatious, to hear him talk as he does——talk *at* you (viz at me) as he does. Ever since my last book has brought me a little more before the public, I can do or say or wish to do and say, nothing right with him—and on, on, he talks epigrams about the sin and shame of those divine angels, called women, daring to tread in the dust of a multitude, when they ought to be minding their clouds. All this, not a bit in joke—but gravely and bitterly. Every new review he sees, there is a burst of indignation—and the League-motion, obliquely entertained as it was, wrapt me in a whirlwind.* You know . . . and I tell him, . . . the feeling is all to be analysed into contempt of the sex. It is just that, and no less. For a woman to hang down her head like a lily through life, and 'die of a rose in aromatic pain' at her death,——to sit or lounge as in a Book of Beauty, and be 'defended' by the strong and mighty thinkers on all sides of her, ——this he thinks, is her destiny and glory. It is not the pudding-making and stocking-darning theory—it is more graceful and picturesque. But the *significance* is precisely the same,—and the absurdity a hundred times over, greater. Who makes my pudding, is useful to me,—but who looks languishing in a Book of Beauty, is good for nothing *so far*.

She had been approached by a committee in Leeds to write a poem in opposition to the Corn Laws. Her family strongly disapproved, and much against her will, she refused.

Angry as all this makes me, I am *not*, as you are perhaps aware, a very strong partizan of the Rights-of-woman-side of the argument —at least I have not been, since I was twelve years old. I believe that, considering men and women in the mass, there *is* an *inequality* of intellect, and that it is proved by the very state of things of which gifted women complain; and more than proved by the manner in which their complaint is received by their own sisterhood. At the same time, the argument used by men in this relation, should go no farther than the fact,—and it is cruel and odious to see the yearning they have, not to meet the weakness of women with their manly protection, but to exaggerate that weakness, in order to parade their protection. I know that women (many of them) encourage this tendency by parading their weakness—and it is detestable to my eyes, in an equal degree, on both sides of sex . . .

In 1853 she revised the new edition of her poetry 'very carefully, and made everything better', and her reflections on a spasmodic contemporary written the same year suggest the manner in which she was progressively disciplining her own temperament:

Alexander Smith I know by copious extracts in reviews, and by some MSS once sent to us by friends and readers. Judging from those he must be set down as a true poet in opulence of imagery, but defective, so far (he is said to be very young)* in the intellectual part of poetry. His images are flowers thrown to him by the gods, beautiful and fragrant, but having no root either in Enna or Olympus. There's no unity and holding together, no reality properly so called, no thinking of any kind.

The process bore fruit in the long verse novel *Aurora Leigh* (1856), a brief look at which can be found in the text below. 'When you have read my new book', she wrote, '. . . put away all my other poems and know me only by the new', but although it remains an impressively comprehensive excursion through all kinds of social,

————

*He was in his early twenties

sexual and political matters, it would certainly be as unfortunate to dismiss all that came before as to ignore the work of her later maturity. If the somewhat pious meditations upon romantic love, the *Sonnets from the Portuguese*, have been saved for posterity because of their basic honesty of approach, it is a pity that the parochial prejudices which first greeted Mrs. Browning's 'Italian' poems should have marked them out for chronic neglect. How dare this passionate female libertarian presume to harangue her fellow country*men* about the remote struggle for Italian freedom: this might well encapsulate the response to *Casa Guidi Windows* (published 1856) and *Poems before Congress* (1860). Mrs. Browning was quite aware of her strengths and her limitations, however: witness the first paragraph of the Advertisement to the earlier published volume:

> This poem contains the impressions of the writer upon events in Tuscany of which she was a witness. 'From a window,' the critic may demur. She bows to the objection in the very title of her work. No continuous narrative nor exposition of political philosophy is attempted by her. It is a simple story of personal impressions, whose only value is in the intensity with which they were received, as proving her warm affection for a beautiful and unfortunate country, and the sincerity with which they are related, as indicating her own good faith and freedom from partisanship.

The opening of the poem gives us just a glimpse of that exhilarating, yet assured, fluidity of conception with expression to match, which she manages to sustain in ranging over the representative part which Florence played in its attempt to liberate itself from Austrian backed control:

> I heard last night a little child go singing
>> 'Neath Casa Guidi windows, by the church,
> *O bella liberta, O bella!*—stringing
>> The same words still on notes he went in search
> So high for, you concluded the upspringing

Of such a nimble bird to sky from perch
Must leave the whole bush in a tremble green,
   And that the heart of Italy must beat,
While such a voice had leave to rise serene
   'Twixt church and palace of a Florence street:

The incisive mind that had been and was to go on serving her so well in her social, sexual reflections is effectively applied to the broad political front:

Long live the people! How they lived! and boiled
And bubbled in the cauldron of the street:
   How the young blustered, nor the old recoiled,
And what a thunderous stir of tongues and feet
   Trod flat the palpitating bells and foiled
The joy-guns of their echo, shattering it!
   How down they pulled the Duke's arms everywhere!
How they set new café-signs, to show
   Where patriots might sip ices in pure air—
(The fresh paint smelling somewhat)! To and fro
   How marched the civic guard, and stopped to stare
When boys broke windows in a civic glow!

Reading the whole of this poem, in fact, one is gratified to suppose that whatever debt there was between husband and wife it was by no means all one way: how much of the general character of *Casa Guidi* resonates in the *Ring and the Book*, for example, or the later *Fifine at the Fair*? And in preferring one or two pieces from Mrs Browning's *Poems before Congress* one realizes (despite the few notes to be found at the end of this selection) how the broadly detailed treatment of culpable human frailty is in a sense highlighted, rather than obscured, by even the most clotted of contemporary allusions and provenance:

You'll take back your Grand-duke?
   I made the treaty upon it.

16

Just venture a quiet rebuke;
    Dall' Ongaro write him a sonnet;
Ricasoli gently explain
    Some need of the constitution:
He'll swear to it over again,
    Providing an 'easy solution.'
You'll call back the Grand-duke.

It is a romantic convention to deplore the snatching away from us of an artist just when his or her finest work seemed on the point of being given to the world. Mrs. Browning's career, as I have tried to suggest, involved a progressive refinement upon her talents, yet the *Last Poems*, published posthumously by her grief-worn husband in 1862, do indicate that improved exercise of her passion and satirical intelligence which it is a pity she could not go on to substantiate. The bitter monologue of *Bianca Among the Nightingales*—with its complex emotional play upon a refrain faintly reminiscent of *Catarina to Camoens*—is breathtaking in its divinely sanctioned sexual throbbing and thrusting:

We paled with love, we shook with love,
    We kissed so close we could not vow;
Till Giulio whispered 'Sweet, above
    God's Ever guaranties this Now.'
And through his words the nightingales
    Drove straight and full their long clear call,
Like arrows through heroic mails,
    And love was awful in it all.
The nightingales, the nightingales!

And Bianca displays a comparable, precisely realized passion when reflecting on the woman for whom she had been passed over:

A worthless woman; mere cold clay
    As all false things are: but so fair,
She takes the breath of men away

Who gaze upon her unaware.
I would not play her larcenous tricks
　　To have her looks! She lied and stole,
And spat into my love's pure pyx
　　The rank saliva of her soul.
And still they sing, the nightingales.

Lord Walter's Wife, a brilliant exposé of the cant of attempted seduction, proved such strong stuff that Thackeray refused to publish it in his vastly popular *Cornhill* magazine:

'If a man finds a woman too fair, he means
　　simply adapted too much
To use unlawful and fatal. The praise! —
　　shall I thank you for such?

'Too fair? — not unless you misuse us! and
　　surely if, once in a while,
You attain to it, straightway you call us no
　　longer too fair, but too vile.

Amy's Cruelty proves not to be such after all, but a rigorous analysis of the uncompromising demands involved in an exchange of genuine love.

It is clear, I think, that it would be vulgar to claim a modernity for Elizabeth Barrett Browning simply on account of her candour. That moral fervour, which I touched on earlier, permeates the most outspoken of her works, and the contextual richness augments the acute psychological exercise of her femininity.

SUGGESTIONS FOR FURTHER READING

Collections of Letters, etc.

F. G. Kenyon. ed., *The Letters of Elizabeth Barrett Browning*, 2 vols. London: Smith, Elder, & Co., 1897.

R. W. Barrett Browning, ed., *The Letters of Robert Browning and Elizabeth Barrett 1845-1846*, 2 vols. London: Harper and Brothers, 1899.

Leonard Huxley, ed., *Elizabeth Barrett Browning: Letters to her Sister, 1845-1859*. London: John Murray, [1929].

Dormer Creston, ed., *Andromeda in Wimpole Street: Containing extracts from the Love Letters of Elizabeth and Robert Browning.* London: Eyre & Spottiswoode, [1929].

Betty Miller, ed., *Elizabeth Barrett to Miss Mitford*. London: John Murray, 1954.

Barbara P. McCarthy, ed., *Elizabeth Barrett to Mr. Boyd*. London: John Murray, 1955.

Elvan Kintner, ed., *The Letters of Robert and Elizabeth Barrett Browning 1845-1846*, 2 vols. Cambridge, Mass.: The Belknap Press of Harvard University Press, 1969.

Willard Bissell Pope, ed., *Invisible Friends: The Correspondence of Elizabeth Barrett Browning and Benjamin Robert Haydon 1842-1845*. Cambridge, Mass.: Harvard University Press, 1972.

Peter N. Heydon and Philip Kelley, eds., *Elizabeth Barrett Browning's Letters to Mrs. David Ogilvy 1849-1861*. [London] : John Murray, [1974].

Elizabeth Berridge, ed., *The Barretts at Hope End: The Early Diary of Elizabeth Barrett Browning*. [London] : John Murray, [1974].

Biography and Criticism

Isabel C. Clarke, *Elizabeth Barrett Browning: A Portrait*. London: Hutchinson & Co. Ltd., [undated, published 1929].

Dorothy Hewlett, *Elizabeth Barrett Browning*. London: Cassell and Company Ltd., [1953].

19

Gardner B. Taplin, *The Life of Elizabeth Barrett Browning*. London: John Murray, [1957] .

Alethea Hayter, *Mrs. Browning: A Poet's Work and its Setting*. London: Faber and Faber, [1962] .

Katherine H. Porter, *Through a Glass Darkly: Spiritualism in the Browning Circle*. New York: Octagon Books, 1972.

Virginia L. Radley, *Elizabeth Barrett Browning*. New York: Twayne Publishers, Inc., [1972] . Twayne English Author Series, a useful introduction.

Several specialist articles appear from time to time in the periodicals *Studies in Browning and his circle* (published at Baylor University, Texas, USA) and *Browning Society Notes* (published by the Browning Society of London).

A Note on the Text

The following selections are taken from F. G. Kenyon's edition of *The Poetical Works of Elizabeth Barrett Browning*, London: Smith, Elder, & Co., 1897. This is the 'first complete edition [although one or two pieces have been published since] . . . the text of every poem [being] that of the authoress's latest revision, [4th edition of 1856] so that [being an acute reviser] each poem appears in its most perfect form, although the exhibition of her genius in its several stages of development is thereby somewhat modified.' She went on writing up to her death in 1861 and 'subsequent accretions' after 1856 are, of course, included in the edition.

from THE BATTLE OF MARATHON (1820)

Zeno the bravest of the Persian youth   1275
Renowned for filial piety and truth;
His mother's only joy; she loved to trace
His father's features in his youthful face;
That Sire, in fight o'erwhelmed, mid seas of gore
Slept unentombed, and cared for fame no more.   1280
And now as youth in opening manhood glows,
All his loved father in his visage rose,
Like him, regardful of his future fame,
Resolved like him to immortalize his name,
At glory's call, he quits his native shore   1285
And feeble parent, to return no more;
Oh! what prophetic griefs her bosom wrung
When on his neck in agony she hung!
When on that breast she hid her sorrowing face,
And feared to take, or shun, the last embrace!   1290
Unhappy youth! the fates decree thy doom,
Those flowers, prepared for joy, shall deck thy tomb.
Thy mother now no more shall hail thy name
So high enrolled upon the lists of fame,
Nor check the widow's tear, the widow's sigh,   1295
For e'en her son, her Zeno's doom to die.
Zeno, e'en thou! for so the Gods decree,
A parents' threshold opes no more for thee!
On him the hero turned his eye severe
Nor on his visage saw one mark of fear;   1300
There manly grace improved each separate part,
And joined by ties of truth, the face and heart.
The supple javelin then the Grecian tries
With might gigantic, and the youth defies.
Its point impetuous, at his breast he flung,   1305

21

The brazen shield received, and mocking rung;
Then Zeno seized the lance, the Chief defied,
And scoffing, thus began, in youthful pride;
'Go, mighty Greek! to weaker warriors go,
And fear this arm, and an unequal foe;   1310
A mother gave the mighty arms I bear,
Nor think with such a gift, I cherish fear.'
He hurled the lance, but Pallas' self was there,
And turned the point, it passed in empty air.
With hope renewed, again the hero tries   1315
His boasted might, the thirsty weapon flies
In Zeno's breast it sinks, and drank the gore,
And stretched the hero vanquished on the shore;
Gasping for utterance, and life and breath,
For fame he sighs, nor fears approaching death.   1320
Themistocles perceived, and bending low
Thought of his friends, and tears began to flow
That washed the bleeding bosom of his foe.
Young Zeno then, the Grecian hero eyed
Rejects his offered aid, and all defied,   1325
Breathed one disdainful sigh, and turned his head and died.

from AN ESSAY ON MIND (1826)

Though analyzing Truth must still divide   440
Historic state, and scientific pride;
Yet one stale fact, our judging thoughts infer—
Since each is human, each is prone to err!
Oft, in the night of Time, doth History stray,
And lift her lantern, and proclaim it day!   445
And oft, when day's eternal glories shine,

Doth Science, boasting, cry—'The light is mine!'
So hard to bear, with unobstructed sight,   (k)
Th'excess of darkness, or th'extreme of light.

Yet, to be just, though faults belong to each,   450
The themes of one, an humbler moral teach:
And, 'midst th'historian's eloquence, and skill,
The human chronicler is human still.
If on past power, his eager thoughts be cast,
It brings an awful antidote—'tis past!   455
If, deathless fame, his ravish'd organs scan,
The deathless fame exists for buried man:
Power, and decay, at once he turns to view;
And, with the strength, beholds the weakness too.
Not so, doth Science' musing son aspire;   460
And pierce creation, with his eye of fire.
Yon mystic pilgrims of the starry way,
No humbling lesson, to his soul, convey;
No tale of change, their changeless course hath taught;
And works divine excite no earthward thought.   465
And still, he, reckless, builds the splendid dream;
And still, his pride increases with his theme;
And still, the cause is slighted in th'effect;
And still, self-worship follows self-respect.
Too apt to watch the engines of the scene,   470
And lose the hand, which moves the vast machine;
View Matter's form, and not its moving soul;
Interpret parts, and misconceive the whole:
While, darkly musing 'twixt the earth, and sky,
His heart grows narrow, as his hopes grow high;   475
And quits, for aye, with unavailing loss,
The sympathies of earth, but not the dross;
Till Time sweeps down the fabric of his trust;
And life, and riches, turn to death, and dust.

23

[. . .]
Hence let our Poets, with discerning glance,
Forbear to imitate the stage of France.
What though Corneille arouse the thrilling chords,
And walk with Genius o'er th'inspired boards;
What though his rival bring, with calmer grace,   1065
The classic unities of time and place,—
All polish, and all eloquence—'twere mean
To leave the path of Nature for Racine;
When Nero's parent, 'midst her woe, defines
The wrong that tortures—in two hundred lines: 1070
Or when Orestes, madden'd by his crime,
Forgets life, joy, and everything—but rhyme.

   While thus to character and nature, true,
Still keep the harmony of verse in view;
Yet not in changeless concord,—it should be   1075
Though graceful, nervous,—musical, though free;
Not clogg'd by useless drapery, not beset
By the superfluous word, or epithet,
Wherein Conception only dies in state,
As Draco, smother'd by the garments' weight—   1080
But join, Amphion-like, (whose magic fire
Won the deep music of the Maian lyre,
To call Boeotia's city from the ground.)
The just in structure, with the sweet in sound.

[. . .]
   And oh! while thus the spirit glides away,—
Give to the world its memory with its clay!
Some page our country's grateful eyes may scan;   1255
Some useful truth to bless surviving man;
Some name to honest bosoms justly dear;
Some grave t'exalt the thought, and claim the tear;

24

So when the pilgrim Sun is travelling o'er
The last blue hill, to gild a distant shore, 1260
He leaves a freshness in the evening scene,
That tells Creation where his steps have been!

[*POEMS* 1844]
THE SOUL'S EXPRESSION

With stammering lips and insufficient sound
I strive and struggle to deliver right
That music of my nature, day and night
With dream and thought and feeling interwound,
And inly answering all the senses round
With octaves of a mystic depth and height
Which step out grandly to the infinite
From the dark edges of the sensual ground.
This song of soul I struggle to outbear
Through portals of the sense, sublime and whole,
And utter all myself into the air;
But if I did it,—as the thunder–roll
Breaks its own cloud, my flesh would perish there,
Before that dread apocalypse of soul.

LADY GERALDINE'S COURTSHIP
A Romance of the Age

A Poet writes to his Friend. Place—*A Room in Wycombe Hall.*
Time—*Late in the evening.*

I.

Dear my friend and fellow-student, I would lean my spirit o'er you!
Down the purple of this chamber tears should scarcely run at will.
I am humbled who was humble. Friend, I bow my head before you:
You should lead me to my peasants, but their faces are too still.

II.

There's a lady, an earl's daughter,—she is proud and she is noble,
And she treads the crimson carpet amd she breathes the perfumed
   air,   6
And a kingly blood sends glances up, her princely eye to trouble,
And the shadow of a monarch's crown is softened in her hair.

III.

She has halls among the woodlands, she has castles by the breakers,
She has farms and she has manors, she can threaten and command:
And the palpitating engines snort in steam across her acres,   11
As they mark upon the blasted heaven the measure of the land.

IV.

There are none of England's daughters who can show a prouder
   presence;
Upon princely suitors' praying she has looked in her disdain.   14
She was sprung of English nobles, I was born of English peasants;
What was *I* that I should love her, save for competence to pain?

V.

I was only a poor poet, made for singing at her casement,
As the finches or the thrushes, while she thought of other things.
Oh, she walked so high above me, she appeared to my abasement,
In her lovely silken murmur, like an angel clad in wings!   20

VI.

Many vassals bow before her as her carriage sweeps their doorways;
She has blest their little children, as a priest or queen were she:
Far too tender, or too cruel far, her smile upon the poor was,
For I thought it was the same smile which she used to smile on *me*.

VII.

She has voters in the Commons, she has lovers in the palace,   25
And, of all the fair court-ladies, few have jewels half as fine;

Oft the Prince has named her beauty 'twixt the red wine and the
    chalice: 27
Oh, and what was *I* to love her? my beloved, my Geraldine!

VIII.
Yet I could not choose but love her: I was born to poet-uses,
To love all things set above me, all of good and all of fair. 20
Nymphs of mountain, not of valley, we are wont to call the Muses;
And in nympholeptic climbing, poets pass from mount to star.

IX.
And because I was a poet, and because the public praised me,
With a critical deduction for the modern writer's fault,
I could sit at rich men's tables,—though the courtesies that raised me,
Still suggested clear between us the pale spectrum of the salt. 26

X.
And they praised me in her presence—'Will your book appear this
    summer?'
Then returning to each other—'Yes, our plans are for the moors.'
Then with whisper dropped behind me—'There he is! the latest
    comer.
Oh, she only likes his verses! what is over, she endures. 30

XI.
'Quite low-born, self-educated! somewhat gifted though by nature,
And we make a point of asking him,—of being very kind.
You may speak, he does not hear you! and, besides, he writes no
    satire,—
All these serpents kept by charmers leave the natural sting behind.'

XII.
I grew scornfuller, grew colder, as I stood up there among them,
Till as frost intense will burn you, the cold scorning scorched my
    brow; 46

When a sudden silver speaking, gravely cadenced, over-rung them,
And a sudden silken stirring touched my inner nature through.

XIII.

I looked upward and beheld her: with a calm and regnant spirit,   49
Slowly round she swept her eyelids, and said clear before them all—
'Have you such superfluous honour, sir, that able to confer it
You will come down, Mister Bertram, as my guest to Wycombe Hall?'

XIV.

Here she paused; she had been paler at the first word of her speaking,
But, because a silence followed it, blushed somewhat, as for shame:
Then, as scorning her own feeling, resumed calmly—'I am seeking 55
More distinction than these gentlemen think worthy of my claim.

XV.

'Ne'ertheless, you see, I seek it—not because I am a woman,'
(Here her smile sprang like a fountain and, so, overflowed her mouth)
'But because my woods in Sussex have some purple shades at
     gloaming
Which are worthy of a king in state, or poet in his youth.   60

XVI.

'I invite you, Mister Bertram, to no scene for worldly speeches—
Sir, I scarce should dare—but only where God asked the thrushes
     first:
And if *you* will sing beside them, in the covert of my beeches,
I will thank you for the woodlands,—for the human world at worst.'

XVII.

Then she smiled around right childly, then she gazed around right
     queenly,   65
And I bowed—I could not answer;alternated light and gloom—
While as one who quells the lions, with a steady eye serenely,
She, with level fronting eyelids, passed out stately from the room.

XVIII.

Oh, the blessèd woods of Sussex, I can hear them still around me,
With their leafy tide of greenery still rippling up the wind!   70
Oh the cursed woods of Sussex! where the hunter's arrow found me,
When a fair face and a tender voice had made me mad and blind!

XIX.

In that ancient hall of Wycombe thronged the numerous guests
     invited,
And the lovely London ladies trod the doors with gliding feet;
And their voices low with fashion, not with feeling, softly
     freighted   75
All the air about the windows with elastic laughters sweet.

XX.

For at eve the open windows flung their light out on the terrace
Which the floating orbs of curtains did with gradual shadow sweep,
While the swans upon the river, fed at morning by the heiress,
Trembled downward through their snowy wings at music in their
     sleep.   80

XXI.

And there evermore was music, both of instrument and singing,
Till the finches of the shrubberies grew restless in the dark;
But the cedars stood up motionless, each in a moonlight's
     ringing,
And the deer, half in the glimmer, strewed the hollows of the park.

XXII.

And though sometimes she would bind me with her silver-corded
     speeches   85
To commix my words and laughter with the converse and the jest,
Oft I sat apart and, gazing on the river through the beeches,
Heard, as pure the swans swam down it, her pure voice o'erfloat
     the rest.

XXIII.

In the morning, horn of huntsman, hoof of steed and laugh of rider,
Spread out cheery from the courtyard till we lost them in the hills,
While herself and other ladies, and her suitors left beside her,   91
Went a-wandering up the gardens through the laurels and abeles.

XXIV.

Thus, her foot upon the new-mown grass, bareheaded, with the
    flowing
Of the virginal white vesture gathered closely to her throat,
And the golden ringlets in her neck just quickened by her going,
And appearing to breathe sun for air, and doubting if to float,—

XXV.

With a bunch of dewy maple, which her right hand held above her,
And which trembled a green shadow in betwixt her and the skies,
And she turned her face in going, thus, she drew me on to love her,
And to worship the divineness of the smile hid in her eyes.   100

XXVI.

For her eyes alone smile constantly; her lips have serious sweetness,
And her front is calm, the dimple rarely ripples on the cheek;
But her deep blue eyes smile constantly, as if they in discreetness
Kept the secret of a happy dream she did not care to speak.

XXVII.

Thus she drew me the first morning, out across into the garden,
And I walked among her noble friends and could not keep behind.
Spake she unto all and unto me—'Behold, I am the warden   107
Of the song-birds in these lindens, which are cages to their mind.

XXVIII.

'But within this swarded circle into which the lime-walk brings us,
Where the beeches, rounded greenly, stand away in reverent fear, 110

I will let no music enter, saving what the fountain sings us
Which the lilies round the basin may seem pure enough to hear.

XXIX.

'The live air that waves the lilies waves the slender jet of water
Like a holy thought sent feebly up from soul of fasting saint:
Whereby lies a marble Silence, sleeping (Lough the sculptor wrought
    her),   115
So asleep she is forgetting to say Hush!—a fancy quaint.

XXX.

'Mark how heavy white her eyelids! not a dream between them
    lingers:
And the left hand's index droppeth from the lips upon the cheek:
While the right hand,—with the symbol-rose held slack within the
    fingers,—   119
Has fallen backward in the basin—yet this Silence will not speak!

XXXI.

'That the essential meaning growing may exceed the special symbol,
Is the thought as I conceive it: it applies more high and low.
Our true noblemen will often through right nobleness grow humble,
And assert an inward honour by denying outward show.'

XXXII.

'Nay, your Silence,' said I, 'truly, holds her symbol-rose but slackly,
Yet *she holds it*, or would scarcely be a Silence to our ken: 126
And your nobles wear their ermine on the outside, or walk blackly
In the presence of the social law as mere ignoble men.

XXXIII.

'Let the poets dream such dreaming! madam, in these British
    islands   129
'Tis the substance that wanes ever, 'tis the symbol that exceeds.

Soon we shall have nought but symbol: and, for statues like this Silence,
    Shall accept the rose's image—in another case, the weed's.'

XXXIV.
'Not so quickly,' she retorted.—'I confess, where'er you go, you
Find for things, names—shows for actions, and pure gold for honour clear:
But when all is run to symbol in the Social, I will throw you   135
The world's book which now reads dryly, and sit down with Silence here.'

XXXV.
Half in playfulness she spoke, I thought, and half in indignation;
Friends who listened, laughed her words off, while her lovers deemed her fair:
A fair woman, flushed with feeling, in her noble-lighted station
Near the statue's white reposing—and both bathed in sunny air!

XXXVI.
With the trees round, not so distant but you heard their vernal murmur,   141
And beheld in light and shadow the leaves in and outward move,
And the little fountain leaping toward the sun-heart to be warmer,
Then recoiling in a tremble from the too much light above.

XXXVII.
'Tis a picture for remembrance. And thus, morning after morning,
Did I follow as she drew me by the spirit to her feet.   146
Why, her greyhound followed also! dogs—we both were dogs for scorning—
To be sent back when she pleased it and her path lay through the wheat.

XXXVIII.

And thus, morning after morning, spite of vows and spite of sorrow,
Did I follow at her drawing, while the week-days passed along,— 150
Just to feed the swans this noontide, or to see the fawns to-morrow,
Or to teach the hill-side echo some sweet Tuscan in a song.

XXXIX.

Ay, for sometimes on the hill-side, while we sate down in the
    gowans,
With the forest green behind us and its shadow cast before,
And the river running under, and across it from the rowans   155
A brown partridge whirring near us till we felt the air it bore,—

XL.

There, obedient to her praying, did I read aloud the poems
Made to Tuscan flutes, or instruments more various of our own;
Read the pastoral parts of Spenser, or the subtle interflowings
Found in Petrarch's sonnets—here's the book, the leaf is folded
    down!   160

XLI.

Or at times a modern volume, Wordsworth's solemn-thoughted idyl,
Howitt's ballad-verse, or Tennyson's enchanted reverie,—
Or from Browning some 'Pomegranate', which, if cut deep down
    the middle,
Shows a heart within blood-tinctured, of a veined humanity.

XLII.

Or at times I read there, hoarsely, some new poem of my making:
Poets ever fail in reading their own verses to their worth,   166
For the echo in you breaks upon the words which you are speaking,
And the chariot wheels jar in the gate through which you drive them
    forth.

XLIII.

After, when we were grown tired of books, the silence round us
    flinging   169
A slow arm of sweet compression, felt with beatings at the breast,
She would break out on a sudden in a gush of woodland singing,
Like a child's emotion in a god—a naiad tired of rest.

XLIV.

Oh, to see or hear her singing! scarce I know which is divinest,
For her looks sing too—she modulates her gestures on the tune,
And her mouth stirs with the song, like song; and when the notes
    are finest,   175
'Tis the eyes that shoot out vocal light and seem to swell them on.

XLV.

Then we talked—oh, how we talked! her voice, so cadenced in the
    talking,
Made another singing—of the soul! a music without bars:
While the leafy sounds of woodlands, humming round where we
    were walking,   179
Brought interposition worthy-sweet,—as skies about the stars.

XLVI.

And she spake such good thoughts natural, as if she always thought
    them;
She had sympathies so rapid, open, free as bird on branch,
Just as ready to fly east as west, whichever way besought them,
In the birchen-wood a chirrup, or a cock-crow in the grange.

XLVII.

In her utmost lightness there is truth—and often she speaks lightly,
Has a grace in being gay which even mournful souls approve,   186
For the root of some grave earnest thought is understruck so lightly
As to justify the foliage and the waving flowers above.

XLVIII.

And she talked on—*we* talked rather! upon all things, substance,
    shadow,
Of the sheep that browsed the grasses, of the reapers in the corn,
Of the little children from the schools, seen winding through the
    meadow,   191
Of the poor rich world beyond them, still kept poorer by its scorn.

XLIX.

So, of men, and so, of letters—books are men of higher stature,
And the only men that speak aloud for future times to hear;
So, of mankind in the abstract, which grows slowly into nature,
Yet will lift the cry of 'progress', as it trod from sphere to
    sphere.   196

L.

And her custom was to praise me when I said,—'The Age culls
    simples,
With a broad clown's back turned broadly to the glory of the stars.
We are gods by our own reck'ning, and may well shut up the
    temples,   199
And wield on, amid the incense-steam, the thunder of our cars.

LI.

'For we throw out acclamations of self-thanking, self-admiring,
With, at every mile run faster,—"O the wondrous wondrous age!"
Little thinking if we work our SOULS as nobly as our iron,
Or if angels will commend us at the goal of pilgrimage.

LII.

'Why, what *is* this patient entrance into nature's deep resources
But the child's most gradual learning to walk upright without bane!
When we drove out, from the cloud of steam, majestical white
    horses,   207
Are we greater than the first men who led black ones by the mane?

LIII.

'If we trod the deeps of ocean, if we struck the stars in rising,
If we wrapped the globe intensely with one hot electric breath,
'Twere but power within our tether, no new spirit-power comprising,
And in life we were not greater men, nor bolder men in death.'

LIV.

She was patient with my teasing; and I loved her, loved her certes
As I loved all heavenly objects, with uplifted eyes and hands;
As I loved pure inspirations, loved the graces, loved the virtues,
In a Love content with writing his own name on desert sands.   216

LV.

Or at least I thought so, purely; thought no idiot Hope was raising
Any crown to crown Love's silence, silent Love that sate alone:
Out, alas! the stag is like me, he that tries to go on grazing
With the great deep gun-wound in his neck, then reels with sudden
        moan.   220

LVI.

It was thus I reeled. I told you that her hand had many suitors;
But she smiles them down imperially as Venus did the waves,
And with such a gracious coldness that they cannot press their
        futures
On the present of her courtesy, which yieldingly enslaves.

LVII.

And this morning as I sat alone within the inner chamber   225
With the great saloon beyond it, lost in pleasant thought serene,
For I had been reading Camoëns, that poem you remember,
Which his lady's eyes are praised in as the sweetest ever seen.

LVIII.

And the book lay open, and my thought flew from it, taking from it
A vibration and impulsion to an end beyond its own,   230

As the branch of a green osier, when a child would overcome it,
Springs up freely from his claspings and goes swinging in the sun.

LIX.
As I mused I heard a murmur; it grew deep as it grew longer,
Speakers using earnest language—'Lady Geraldine, you *would!*'
And I heard a voice that pleaded, ever on in accents stronger,   235
As a sense of reason gave it power to make its rhetoric good.

LX.
Well I knew that voice; it was an earl's, of soul that matched his
  station,
Soul completed into lordship, might and right read on his brow;
Very finely courteous; far too proud to doubt his domination
Of the common people, he atones for grandeur by a bow.   240

LXI.
High straight forehead, nose of eagle, cold blue eyes of less
  · expression
Than resistance, coldly casting off the looks of other men,
As steel, arrows; unelastic lips which seem to taste possession
And be cautious lest the common air should injure or distrain.

LXII.
For the rest, accomplished, upright,—ay, and standing by his order
With a bearing not ungraceful; fond of art and letters too;   246
Just a good man made a proud man,—as the sandy rocks that border
A wild coast, by circumstances, in a regnant ebb and flow.

LXIII.
Thus, I knew that voice, I heard it, and I could not help the
  hearkening:
In the room I stood up blindly, and my burning heart within   250

Seemed to seethe and fuse my senses till they ran on all sides darkening,
And scorched, weighed like melted metal round my feet that
    stood therein.

    LXIV.

And that voice, I heard it pleading, for love's sake, for wealth,
    position,
For the sake of liberal uses and great actions to be done: 254
And she interrupted gently, 'Nay, my lord, the old tradition
Of your Normans, by some worthier hand than mine is, should
    be won.'

    LXV.

'Ah, that white hand!' he said quickly,—and in his he either drew it
Or attempted—for with gravity and instance she replied,
'Nay, indeed, my lord, this talk is vain, and we had best eschew it
And pass on, like friends, to other points less easy to decide.'   260

    LXVI.

What he said again, I know not: it is likely that his trouble
Worked his pride up to the surface, for she answered in slow scorn,
'And your lordship judges rightly. Whom I marry shall be noble,
Ay, and wealthy. I shall never blush to think how he was born.'

    LXVII.

There, I maddened! her words stung me. Life swept through me into
    fever,   265
And my soul sprang up astonished, sprang full-statured in an hour.
Know you what it is when anguish, with apocalyptic NEVER,
To a Pythian height dilates you, and despair sublimes to power?

    LXVIII.

From my brain the soul-wings budded, waved a flame about my
    body,

Whence convention coiled to ashes. I felt self-drawn out, as man,
From amalgamate false natures, and I saw the skies grow ruddy   271
With the deepening feet of angels, and I knew what spirits can.

LXIX.
I was mad, inspired—say either! (anguish worketh inspiration)
Was a man or beast—perhaps so, for the tiger roars when speared;
And I walked on, step by step along the level of my passion—   275
Oh my soul! and passed the doorway to her face, and never feared.

LXX.
He had left her, peradventure, when my foot-step proved my coming,
But for *her*—she half arose, then sate, grew scarlet and grew pale.
Oh, she trembled! 'tis so always with a worldly man or woman
In the presence of true spirits: what else *can* they do but quail?   280

LXXI.
Oh, she fluttered like a tame bird, in among its forest brothers
Far too strong for it; then drooping, bowed her face upon her hands;
And I spake out wildly, fiercely, brutal truths of her and others:
I, she planted in the desert, swathed her, windlike, with my sands.

LXXII.
I plucked up her social fictions, bloody-rooted though leaf-verdant,
Trod them down with words of shaming,—all the purple and the gold,
All the 'landed stakes' and lordships, all that spirits pure and ardent
Are cast out of love and honour because chancing not to hold.

LXIII.
'For myself I do not argue,' said I, 'though I love you, madam,
But for better souls that nearer to the height of yours have trod: 290
And this age shows, to my thinking, still more infidels to Adam
Than directly, by profession, simple infidels to God.

LXXIV.

'Yet, O God,' I said, 'O grave,' I said, 'O mother's heart and bosom,
With whom first and last are equal, saint and corpse and little child!
We are fools to your deductions, in these figments of heart-closing;
We are traitors to your causes, in these sympathies defiled.   296

LXXV.

'Learn more reverence, madam, not for rank or wealth—*that* needs
   no learning:
That comes quickly, quick as sin does, ay, and culminates to sin;
But for Adam's seed, MAN! Trust me, 'tis a clay above your scorning,
With God's image stamped upon it, and God's kindling breath
   within.   300

LXXVI.

'What right have you, madam, gazing in your palace mirror daily,
Getting so by heart your beauty which all others must adore,
While you draw the golden ringlets down your fingers, to vow gaily
You will wed no man that's only good to God, and nothing more?

LXXVII.

'Why, what right have you, made fair by that same God, the sweetest
   woman   305
Of all women He has fashioned, with your lovely spirit-face
Which would seem too near to vanish if its smile were not so human,
And your voice of holy sweetness, turning common words to grace,—

LXXVIII.

'What right *can* you have, God's other works to scorn, despise,
   revile them
In the gross, as mere men, broadly—not as *noble* men, forsooth,—
As mere Pariahs of the outer world, forbidden to assoil them
In the hope of living, dying, near that sweetness of your mouth?

LXXIX.

'Have you any answer, madam? If my spirit were less earthly,
If its instrument were gifted with a better silver string,
I would kneel down where I stand, and say—Behold me! I am
    worthy   315
Of thy loving, for I love thee. I am worthy as a king.

LXXX.

'As it is—your ermined pride, I swear, shall feel this stain upon her,
That *I*, poor, weak, tost with passion, scorned by me and you again,
Love you, madam, dare to love you, to my grief and your dishonour,
To my endless desolation, and your impotent disdain!'   320

LXXXI.

More mad words like these—mere madness! friend, I need not write
    them fuller,
For I hear my hot soul dropping on the lines in showers of tears.
Oh, a woman! friend, a woman! why, a beast had scarce been duller
Than roar bestial loud complaints against the shining of the spheres.

LXXXII.

But at last there came a pause. I stood all vibrating with thunder 325
Which my soul had used. The silence drew her face up like a call.
Could you guess what word she uttered? She looked up, as if in
    wonder,
With tears beaded on her lashes, and said-'Bertram!'—It was all.

LXXXIII.

If she had cursed me, and she might have, or if even, with queenly
    bearing
Which at need is used by women, she had risen up and said,   330
'Sir, you are my guest, and therefore I have given you a full hearing.
Now, beseech you, choose a name exacting somewhat less,
    instead!'—

LXXXIV.

I had borne it: but that 'Bertram'—why, it lies there on the paper
A mere word, without her accent, and you cannot judge the weight
Of the calm which crushed my passion: I seemed drowning in a
    vapour;   335
And her gentleness destroyed me whom her scorn made desolate.

LXXXV.

So, struck backward and exhausted by that inward flow of passion
Which had rushed on, sparing nothing, into forms of abstract truth,
By a logic agonising through unseemly demonstration,
And by youth's own anguish turning grimly grey the hairs of
    youth,—   340

LXXXVI.

By the sense accursed and instant, that if even I spake wisely
I spake basely—using truth, if what I spake indeed was true,
To avenge the wrong on a woman—*her*, who sate there weighing
    nicely
A poor manhood's worth, found guilty of such deeds as I could do!—

LXXXVII.

By such wrong and woe exhausted—what I suffered and occasioned,—
As a wild horse through a city runs with lightning in his eyes,   346
And then dashing at a church's cold and passive wall, impassioned,
Strikes the death into his burning brain, and blindly drops and dies—

LXXXVIII.

So I fell, struck down before her—do you blame me, friend, for
    weakness?   349
'Twas my strength of passion slew me!—fell before her like a stone;
Fast the dreadful world rolled from me on its roaring wheels of
    blackness:
When the light came I was lying in this chamber and alone.

LXXXIX.

Oh, of course she charged her lacqueys to bear out the sickly burden,
And to cast it from her scornful sight, but not *beyond* the gate:
She is too kind to be cruel, and too haughty not to pardon   355
Such a man as I; 'twere something to be level to her hate.

XC.

But for me—you now are conscious why, my friend, I write this
    letter,
How my life is read all backward, and the charm of life undone.
I shall leave her house at dawn; I would tonight, if I were better—
And I charge my soul to hold my body strengthened for the sun.

XCI.

When the sun has dyed the oriel, I depart, with no last gazes,   361
No weak moanings (one word only, left in writing for her hands),
Out of reach of all derision, and some unavailing praises,
To make front against this anguish in the far and foreign lands.

XCII.

Blame me not. I would not squander life in grief—I am abstemious.
I but nurse my spirit's falcon that its wing may soar again.   366
There's no room for tears of weakness in the blind eyes of a Phemius:
Into work the poet kneads them, and he does not die *till then*.

CONCLUSION

I.

Bertram finished the last pages, while along the silence ever
Still in hot and heavy splashes fell the tears on every leaf.   370
Having ended, he leans backwards in his chair, with lips that quiver
From the deep unspoken, ay, and deep unwritten thoughts of grief.

43

II.

Soh! how still the lady standeth! 'Tis a dream—a dream of mercies!
'Twixt the purple lattice-curtains how she standeth still and pale!
'Tis a vision, sure, of mercies, sent to soften his self-curses,   375
Sent to sweep a patient quiet o'er the tossing of his wail.

III.

'Eyes,' he said, 'now throbbing through me! are ye eyes that did
    undo me?
Shining eyes, like antique jewels set in Parian statue-stone!
Underneath that calm white forehead are ye ever burning torrid
O'er the desolate sand-desert of my heart and life undone?'   380

IV.

With a murmurous stir uncertain, in the air the purple curtain
Swelleth in and swelleth out around her motionless pale brows,
While the gliding of the river sends a rippling noise for ever
Through the open casement whitened by the moonlight's slant
    repose.

V.

Said he—'Vision of a lady! stand there silent, stand there steady!
Now I see it plainly, plainly now I cannot hope or doubt—   386
There, the brows of mild repression—there, the lips of silent
    passion,
Curvèd like an archer's bow to send the bitter arrows out.'

VI.

Ever, evermore the while in a slow silence she kept smiling,
And approached him slowly, slowly, in a gliding measured pace;
With her two white hands extended as if praying one offended,
And a look of supplication gazing earnest in his face.   392

44

VII.

Said he—'Wake me by no gesture,—sound of breath, or stir of vesture!
Let the blessèd apparition melt not yet to its divine!   394
No approaching—hush, no breathing! or my heart must swoon to death in
    death in
The too utter life thou bringest, O thou dream of Geraldine!'

VIII.

Ever, evermore the while in a slow silence she kept smiling,
But the tears ran over lightly from her eyes and tenderly :—
'Dost thou, Bertram, truly love me? Is no woman far above me
Found more worthy of thy poet-heart than such as one as *I*?'   400

IX.

Said he—'I would dream so ever, like the flowing of that river,
Flowing ever in a shadow greenly onward to the sea!
So, thou vision of all sweetness, princely to a full completeness
Would my heart and life flow onward, deathward, through this
    dream of THEE!'

X.

Ever, evermore the while in a slow silence she kept smiling,   405
While the silver tears ran faster down the blushing of her cheeks;
Then with both her hands enfolding both of his, she softly told him,
'Bertram, if I say I love thee, . . . 'tis the vision only speaks.'

XI.

Softened, quickened to adore her, on his knee he fell before her,
And she whispered low in triumph, 'It shall be as I have sworn.   410
Very rich he is in virtues, very noble—noble, certes;
And I shall not blush in knowing that men call him lowly born.'

THE LOST BOWER

I.

In the pleasant orchard-closes,
'God bless all our gains,' say we,
But 'May God bless all our losses'
Better suits with our degree.
Listen, gentle—ay, and simple! listen, children on the knee!

II.

Green the land is where my daily
Steps in jocund childhood played,
Dimpled close with hill and valley,
Dappled very close with shade:
Summer-snow of apple-blossoms running up from glade to glade.

III.

There is one hill I see nearer   11
In my vision of the rest;
And a little wood seems clearer
As it climbeth from the west,
Sideway from the tree-locked valley, to the airy upland crest.

IV.

Small the wood is, green with hazels,
And, completing the ascent,
Where the wind blows and sun dazzles,
Thrills in leafy tremblement,
Like a heart that after climbing beateth quickly through content.

V.

Not a step the wood advances   21
O'er the open hill-top's bound;
There, in green arrest, the branches

46

See their image on the ground:
You may walk beneath them smiling, glad with sight and glad with
    sound.

VI.

For you hearken on your right hand,
How the birds do leap and call
In the greenwood, out of sight and
Out of reach and fear of all;
And the squirrels crack the filberts through their cheerful madrigal.

VII.

On your left, the sheep are cropping   31
The slant grass and daisies pale,
And five apple-trees stand dropping
Separate shadows toward the vale
Over which, in choral silence, the hills look you their 'All hail!'

VIII.

Far out, kindled by each other,
Shining hills on hills arise,
Close as brother leans to brother
When they press beneath the eyes
Of some father praying blessings from the gifts of paradise.

IX.

While beyond, above them mounted,   41
And above their woods alsò,
Malvern hills, for mountains counted
Not unduly, loom a-row—
Keepers of Piers Plowman's visions through the sunshine and the
    snow.

X.

Yet, in childhood, little prized I
That fair walk and far survey;
'Twas a straight walk unadvised by
The least mischief worth a nay;
Up and down—as dull as grammar on the eve of holiday.

XI.

But the wood, all close and clenching   51
Bough in bough and root in root,—
No more sky (for overbranching)
At your head than at your foot,—
Oh, the wood drew me within it by a glamour past dispute!

XII.

Few and broken paths showed through it,
Where the sheep had tried to run,—
Forced with snowy wool to strew it
Round the thickets, when anon
They, with silly thorn-pricked noses, bleated back into the sun.

XIII.

But my childish heart beat stronger   61
Than those thickets dared to grow:
I could pierce them! *I* could longer
Travel on, methought, than so:
Sheep for sheep-paths! braver children climb and creep where they
        would go.

XIV.

And the poets wander, said I,
Over places all as rude:
Bold Rinaldo's lovely lady
Sat to meet him in a wood:
Rosalinda, like a fountain, laughed out pure with solitude.

XV.

And if Chaucer had not travelled   71
Through a forest by a well,
He had never dreamt nor marvelled
At those ladies fair and fell
Who lived smiling without loving in their island-citadel.

XVI.

Thus I thought of the old singers
And took courage from their song,
Till my little struggling fingers
Tore asunder gyve and thong
Of the brambles which entrapped me, and the barrier branches strong.

XVII.

On a day, such pastime keeping,   81
With a fawn's heart debonair,
Under-crawling, overleaping
Thorns that prick and boughs that beat,
I stood suddenly astonied—I was gladdened unaware.

XVIII.

From the place I stood in, floated
Back the covert dim and close,
And the open ground was coated
Carpet-smooth with grass and moss,
And the blue-bell's purple presence signed it worthily across.

XIX.

Here a linden-tree stood, bright'ning   91
All adown its silver rind;
For as some trees draw the lightning,
So this tree, unto my mind,
Drew to earth the blessèd sunshine from the sky where it was shrined.

XX.

Tall the linden-tree, and near it
An old hawthorn also grew;
And wood-ivy like a spirit
Hovered dimly round the two,
Shaping thence that bower of beauty which I sing of thus to you.

XXI.

'Twas a bower for garden fitter   101
Than for any woodland wide:
Though a fresh and dewy glitter
Struck it through from side to side,
Shaped and shaven was the freshness, as by garden-cunning plied.

XXII.

Oh, a lady might have come there,
Hooded fairly like her hawk,
With a book or lute in summer,
And a hope of sweeter talk,—
Listening less to her own music than for footsteps on the walk!

XXIII.

But that bower appeared a marvel   111
In the wildness of the place;
With such seeming art and travail,
Finely fixed and fitted was
Leaf to leaf, the dark-green ivy, to the summit from the base.

XXIV.

And the ivy veined and glossy
Was enwrought with eglantine:
And the wild hop fibred closely,
And the large-leaved columbine,
Arch of door and window-mullion, did right sylvanly entwine.

50

XXV.

Rose-trees either side the door were 121
Growing lithe and growing tall,
Each one set a summer warder
For the keeping of the hall,—
With a red rose and a white rose, leaning nodding at the wall.

XXVI.

As I entered, mosses hushing
Stole all noises from my foot;
And a green elastic cushion,
Clasped within the linden root,
Took me in a chair of silence very rare and absolute.

XXVII.

All the floor was paved with glory, 131
Greenly, silently inlaid
(Through quick motions made before me)
With fair counterparts in shade
Of the fair serrated ivy-leaves which slanted overhead.

XXVIII.

'Is such pavement in a palace?'
So I questioned in my thought:
The sun, shining through the chalice
Of the red rose hung without,
Threw within a red libation, like an answer to my doubt.

XXIX.

At the same time, on the linen 141
Of my childish lap there fell
Two white may-leaves, downward winning
Through the ceiling's miracle,
From a blossom, like an angel, out of sight yet blessing well.

XXX.
Down to floor and up to ceiling
Quick I turned my childish face,
With an innocent appealing
For the secret of the place
To the trees, which surely knew it in partaking of the grace.

XXXI.
Where's no foot of human creature 151
How could reach a human hand?
And if this be work of Nature,
Why has Nature turned so bland,
Breaking off from other wild-work? It was hard to understand.

XXXII.
Was she weary of rough-doing,
Of the bramble and the thorn?
Did she pause in tender rueing
Here of all her sylvan scorn?
Or in mock of Art's deceiving was the sudden mildness worn?

XXXIII.
Or could this same bower (I fancied) 161
Be the work of Dryad strong,
Who surviving all that chancèd
In the world's old pagan wrong,
Lay hid, feeding in the woodland on the last true poet's song?

XXXIV.
Or was this the house of fairies,
Left, because of the rough ways,
Unassoiled by Ave Marys
Which the passing pilgrim prays,
And beyond St. Catherine's chiming on the blessèd Sabbath days?

XXXV.

So, young muser, I sat listening   171
To my fancy's wildest word:
On a sudden, through the glistening
Leaves around, a little stirred,
Came a sound, a sense of music which was rather felt than heard.

XXXVI.

Softly, finely, it inwound me;
From the world it shut me in,—
Like a fountain, falling round me,
Which with silver waters thin
Clips a little water Naiad sitting smilingly within.

XXXVII.

Whence the music came, who knoweth?   181
_I_ know nothing: but indeed
Pan or Faunus never bloweth
So much sweetness from a reed
Which has sucked the milk of waters at the oldest river-head.

XXXVIII.

Never lark the sun can waken
With such sweetness! when the lark,
The high planets overtaking
In the half-evanished Dark,
Casts his singing to their singing, like an arrow to the mark.

XXXIX.

Never nightingale so singeth: 191
Oh, she leans on thorny tree
And her poet-song she flingeth
Over pain to victory!
Yet she never sings such music,—or she sings it not to me.

XL.

Never blackbirds, never thrushes
Nor small finches sing as sweet,
When the sun strikes through the bushes
To their crimson clinging feet,
And their pretty eyes look sideways to the summer heavens complete.

XLI.

If it *were* a bird, it seemèd   201
Most like Chaucer's, which, in sooth,
He of green and azure dreamèd,
While it sat in spirit-ruth
On that bier of a crowned lady, singing nigh her silent mouth.

XLII.

If it *were* a bird?—ah, sceptic,
Give me 'yea' or give me 'nay'—
Though my soul were nympholeptic
As I heard that virèlay,
You may stoop your pride to pardon, for my sin is far away!

XLIII.

I rose up in exaltation   211
And an inward trembling heat,
And (it seemed) in geste of passion
Dropped the music to my feet
Like a garment rustling downwards—such a silence followed it!

XLIV.

Heart and head beat through the quiet
Full and heavily, though slower:
In the song, I think, and by it,
Mystic Presences of power
Had up-snatched me to the Timeless, then returned me to the Hour.

XLV.

In a child-abstraction lifted,   221
Straightway from the bower I past,
Foot and soul being dimly drifted
Through the greenwood, till, at last,
In the hill-top's open sunshine I all consciously was cast.

XLVI.

Face to face with the true mountains
I stood silently and still,
Drawing strength from fancy's dauntings,
From the air about the hill,
And from Nature's open mercies and most debonair goodwill.

XLVII.

Oh, the golden-hearted daisies   231
Witnessed there, before my youth,
To the truth of things, with praises
Of the beauty of the truth;
And I woke to Nature's real, laughing joyfully for both.

XLVIII.

And I said within me, laughing,
I have found a bower to-day,
A green lusus, fashioned half in
Chance and half in Nature's play,
And a little bird sings nigh it, I will nevermore missay.

XLIX.

Henceforth, *I* will be the fairy   241
Of this bower not built by one;
I will go there, sad or merry,
With each morning's benison,
And the bird shall be my harper in the dreamhall I have won.

L.

So I said. But the next morning,
(—Child, look up into my face—
'Ware, oh sceptic, of your scorning!
This is truth in its pure grace!)
The next morning, all had vanished, or my wandering missed the place.

LI.

Bring an oath most sylvan-holy,   251
And upon it swear me true—
By the wind-bells swinging slowly
Their mute curfews in the dew,
By the advent of the snowdrop, by the rosemary and rue,—

LII.

I affirm by all or any,
Let the cause be charm or chance,
That my wandering searches many
Missed the bower of my romance—
That I nevermore upon it turned my mortal countenance.

LIII.

I affirm that, since I lost it,   261
Never bower has seemed so fair:
Never garden-creeper crossed it
With so deft and brave an air,
Never bird sung in the summer, as I saw and heard them there.

LIV.

Day by day, with new desire,
Toward my wood I ran in faith,
Under leaf and over brier,
Through the thickets, out of breath;
Like the prince who rescued Beauty from the sleep as long as death.

LV.

But his sword of mettle clashèd,   271
And his arm smote strong, I ween,
And her dreaming spirit flashèd
Through her body's fair white screen,
And the light therof might guide him up the cedar alleys green:

LVI.

But for me I saw no splendour—
All my sword was my child-heart;
And the wood refused surrender
Of that bower it held apart,
Safe as Œdipus's grave-place 'mid Colonos' olives swart.

LVII.

As Aladdin sought the basements   281
His fair palace rose upon,
And the four-and -twenty casements
Which gave answers to the sun;
So, in 'wilderment of gazing, I looked up and I looked down.

LVIII.

Years have vanished since, as wholly
As the little bower did then;
And you call it tender folly
That such thoughts should come again?
Ah, I cannot change this sighing for your smiling, brother men!

LIX.

For this loss it did prefigure   291
Other loss of better good,
When my soul, in spirit-vigour
And in ripened womanhood,
Fell from visions of more beauty than an arbour in a wood.

LX.

I have lost—oh, many a pleasure,
Many a hope and many a power—
Studious health and merry leisure,
The first dew on the first flower!
But the first of all my losses was the losing of the bower.

LXI.

I have lost the dream of Doing,   301
And the other dream of Done,
The first spring in the pursuing,
The first pride in the Begun,—
First recoil from incompletion, in the face of what is won—

LXII.

Exaltations in the far light
Where some cottage only is;
Mild dejections in the starlight,
Which the sadder-hearted miss;
And the child-cheek blushing scarlet for the very shame of bliss.

LXIII.

I have lost the sound child-sleeping   311
Which the thunder could not break;
Something too of the strong leaping
Of the staglike heart awake,
Which the pale is low for keeping in the road it ought to take.

LXIV.

Some respect to social fictions
Has been also lost by me;
And some generous genuflexions,
Which my spirit offered free
To the pleasant old conventions of our false humanity.

LXV.

All my losses did I tell you,   321
  Ye perchance would look away:—
  Ye would answer me, 'Farewell! you
  Make sad company to-day,
And your tears are falling faster than the bitter words you say.'

LXVI.

For God placed me like a dial
  In the open ground with power,
  And my heart had for its trial
  All the sun and all the shower:
And I suffered many losses,—and my first was of the bower.

LXVII.

Laugh you? If that loss of mine be   331
  Of no heavy-seeming weight—
  When the cone falls from the pine-tree,
  The young children laugh thereat;
Yet the wind that struck it, riseth, and the tempest shall be great.

LXVIII.

One who knew me in my childhood
  In the glamour and the game,
  Looking on me long and mild, would
  Never know me for the same.
Come, unchanging recollections, where those changes overcame!

LXIX.

By this couch I weakly lie on,   341
  While I count my memories,—
  Through the fingers which, still sighing,
  I press closely on mine eyes,—
Clear as once beneath the sunshine, I behold the bower arise.

LXX.
Springs the linden-tree as greenly,
Stroked with light adown its rind;
And the ivy-leaves serenely
Each in either intertwined;
And the rose-trees at the doorway, they have neither grown nor pined.

LXXI.
From those overblown faint roses   351
Not a leaf appeareth shed,
And that little bud discloses
Not a thorn's breadth more of red,
For the winters and the summers which have passed me overhead.

LXXII.
And that music overfloweth,
Sudden sweet, the sylvan eaves:
Thrush or nightingale—who knoweth?
Fay or Faunus—who believes?
But my heart still trembles in me to the trembling of the leaves.

LXXIII.
Is the bower lost, then? who sayeth   361
That the bower indeed is lost?
Hark! my spirit in it prayeth
Through the sunshine and the frost,—
And the prayer preserves it greenly, to the last and uttermost.

LXXIV.
Till another open for me
In God's Eden-land unknown,
With an angel at the doorway,
White with gazing at His Throne;
And a saint's voice in the palm-trees, singing—'All is lost . . . and *won*!'

TO FLUSH, MY DOG

I.

Loving friend, the gift of one
Who her own true faith has run
   Through my lower nature,
Be my benediction said
With hand upon thy head,   5
      Gentle fellow-creature!

II.

Like a lady's ringlets brown,
Flow thy silken ears adown
   Either side demurely
Of thy silver-suited breast   10
Shining out from all the rest
   Of thy body purely.

III.

Darkly brown thy body is,
Till the sunshine striking this
   Alchemise its dulness,   15
When the sleek curls manifold
Flash all over into gold
   With a burnished fulness.

IV.

Underneath my stroking hand,
Startled eyes of hazel bland   20
   Kindling, growing larger,
Up thou leapest with a spring,
Full of prank and curveting,
   Leaping like a charger.

V.

Leap! thy broad tail waves a light,   25
Leap! thy slender feet are bright,
    Canopied in fringes;
Leap! those tasselled ears of thine
Flicker strangely, fair and fine
    Down their golden inches.   30

VI.

Yet, my pretty, sportive friend,
Little is't to such an end
    That I praise thy rareness;
Other dogs may be thy peers
Haply in these drooping ears   35
    And this glossy fairness.

VII.

But of *thee* it shall be said,
This dog watched beside a bed
    Day and night unweary,
Watched within a curtained room   40
Where no sunbeam brake the gloom
    Round the sick and dreary.

VIII.

Roses, gathered for a vase,
In that chamber died apace,
    Beam and breeze resigning;   45
This dog only, waited on,
Knowing that when light is gone
    Love remains for shining.

IX.

Other dogs in thymy dew
Tracked the hares and followed through   50

Sunny moor or meadow;
This dog only, crept and crept
Next a languid cheek that slept,
    Sharing in the shadow.

X.

Other dogs of loyal cheer   55
Bounded at the whistle clear,
    Up the woodside hieing;
This dog only, watched in reach
Of a faintly uttered speech
    Or a louder sighing.   60

XI.

And if one or two quick tears
Dropped upon his glossy ears
    Or a sigh came double,
Up he sprang in eager haste,
Fawning, fondling, breathing fast,   65
    In a tender trouble.

XII.

And this dog was satisfied
If a pale thin hand would glide
    Down his dewlaps sloping,—
Which he pushed his nose within,   70
After,—platforming his chin
    On the palm left open.

XIII.

This dog, if a friendly voice
Call him now to blither choice
    Than such a chamber-keeping,   75
'Come out!' praying from the door,—

Presseth backward as before,
   Up against me leaping.

   XIV.
Therefore to this dog will I,
Tenderly not scornfully,   80
   Render praise and favour:
With my hand upon his head,
Is my benediction said
   Therefore and for ever.

   XV.
And because he loves me so,   85
Better than his kind will do
   Often man or woman,
Give I back more love again
Than dogs often take of men,
   Leaning from my Human.   90

   XVI.
Blessings on thee, dog of mine,
Pretty collars make thee fine.
   Sugared milk make fat thee!
Pleasures wag on in thy tail,
Hands of gentle motion fail   95
   Nevermore, to pat thee!

   XVII.
Downy pillow take thy head,
Silken coverlid bestead,
   Sunshine help thy sleeping!
No fly's buzzing wake thee up,   100
No man break thy purple cup
   Set for drinking deep in.

XVIII.

Whiskered cats arointed flee,
Sturdy stoppers keep from thee
    Cologne distillations;   105
Nuts lie in thy path for stones,
And thy feast-day macaroons
    Turn to daily rations!

XIX.

Mock I thee, in wishing weal?—
Tears are in my eyes to feel   110
    Thou art made so straitly,
Blessing needs must straiten too,—
Little canst thou joy or do,
    Thou who lovest *greatly*.

XX.

Yet be blessèd to the height   115
Of all goods and all delight
    Pervious to thy nature;
Only *loved* beyond that line,
With a love that answers thine,
    Loving fellow-creature!   120

CATARINA TO CAMOENS

(DYING IN HIS ABSENCE ABROAD, AND REFERRING TO THE POEM
IN WHICH HE RECORDED THE SWEETNESS OF HER EYES)

I.

On the door you will not enter,
    I have gazed too long: adieu!
Hope withdraws her peradventure:
    Death is near me,—and not *you*.

Come, O lover,   5
    Close and cover
These poor eyes, you called, I ween,
'Sweetest eyes were ever seen!'

  II.
When I heard you sing that burden
    In my vernal days and bowers,   10
Other praises disregarding,
    I but hearkened that of yours—
        Only saying
        In heart-playing,
'Blessed eyes mine eyes have been,   15
If the sweetest HIS have seen!'

  III.
But all changes.   At this vesper,
    Cold the sun shines down the door.
If you stood there, would you whisper
    'Love, I love you,' as before,—   20
        Death pervading
        Now, and shading
Eyes you sang of, that yestreen,
As the sweetest ever seen?

  IV.
Yes. I think, were you beside them,   25
    Near the bed I die upon,
Though their beauty you denied them,
    As you stood there, looking down,
        You would truly
        Call them duly,   30
For the love's sake found therein,
'Sweetest eyes were ever seen.'

V.

And if *you* looked down upon them,
    And if *they* looked up to *you*,
All the light which has foregone them   35
    Would be gathered back anew:
        They would truly
        Be as duly
Love-transformed to beauty's sheen,
'Sweetest eyes were ever seen.'   40

VI.

But, ah me! you only see me,
    In your thoughts of loving man,
Smiling soft perhaps and dreamy
    Through the wavings of my fan;
        And unweeting   45
        Go repeating,
In your reverie serene,
'Sweetest eyes were ever seen—'

VII.

While my spirit leans and reaches
    From my body still and pale;   50
Fain to hear what tender speech is
    In your love to help my bale.
        O my poet,
        Come and show it!
Come, of latest love, to glean   55
'Sweetest eyes were ever seen.'

VIII.

O my poet, O my prophet,
    When you praised their sweetness so,

Did you think, in singing of it,
   That it might be near to go?   60
      Had you fancies
      From their glances,
That the grave would quickly screen
'Sweetest eyes were ever seen'?

   IX.
No reply.   The fountain's warble   65
   In the courtyard sounds alone.
As the water to the marble
   So my heart falls with a moan
      From love-sighing
      To this dying.   70
Death forerunneth Love to win
'Sweetest eyes were ever seen.'

   X.
Will you come?   When I'm departed
   Where all sweetnesses are hid,
Where thy voice, my tender-hearted,   75
   Will not lift up either lid.
      Cry, O lover,
      Love is over!
Cry, beneath the cypress green,
'Sweetest eyes were ever seen!'   80

   XI.
When the angelus is ringing,
   Near the convent will you walk,
And recall the choral singing
   Which brought angels down our talk?
      Spirit-shriven   85
      I viewed Heaven,

Till you smiled—'Is earth unclean,
Sweetest eyes were ever seen?'

XII.
When beneath the palace-lattice
   You ride slow as you have done,   90
And you see a face there that is
   Not the old familiar one,—
     Will you oftly
     Murmur softly,
'Here ye watched me morn and e'en,   95
Sweetest eyes were ever seen!'

XIII.
When the palace-ladies, sitting
   Round your gittern, shall have said,
'Poet, sing those verses written
   For the lady who is dead,'   100
     Will you tremble
.   Yet dissemble,—
Or sing hoarse, with tears between,
'Sweetest eyes were ever seen'?

XIV.
'Sweetest eyes!' how sweet in flowings   105
   The repeated cadence is!
Though you sang a hundred poems,
   Still the best one would be this.
     I can hear it
     'Twixt my spirit   110
And the earth-noise intervene—
'Sweetest eyes were ever seen!'

XV.

But the priest waits for the praying,
   And the choir are on their knees,
And the soul must pass away in 115
   Strains more solemn-high than these.
     Miserere
     For the weary!
Oh, no longer for Catrine
'Sweetest eyes were ever seen!' 120

XVI.

Keep my riband, take and keep it,
   (I have loosed it from my hair)
Feeling, while you overweep it,
   Not alone in your despair,
     Since with saintly 125
     Watch unfaintly
Out of heaven shall o'er you lean
'Sweetest eyes were ever seen.'

XVII.

But—but *now*—yet unremovèd
   Up to heaven, they glisten fast; 130
You may cast away, Belovèd,
   In your future all my past:
     Such old phrases
     May be praises
For some fairer bosom-queen— 135
'Sweetest eyes were ever seen!'

XVIII.

Eyes of mine, what are ye doing?
   Faithless, faithless,—praised amiss
If a tear be of your showing,

Dropt for any hope of HIS!   140
   Death has boldness
   Beside coldness,
If unworthy tears demean
'Sweetest eyes were ever seen.'

XIX.
I will look out to his future;   145
   I will bless it till it shine.
Should he ever be a suitor
   Unto sweeter eyes than mine,
      Sunshine gold them,
      Angels shield them,   150
Whatsoever eyes terrene
Be the sweetest HIS have seen!

WINE OF CYPRUS

GIVEN TO ME BY H. S. BOYD, AUTHOR OF 'SELECTED PASSAGES FROM THE GREEK FATHERS,' ETC., TO WHOM THESE STANZAS ARE ADDRESSED.

I.

If old Bacchus were the speaker,
    He would tell you with a sigh
Of the Cyprus in this beaker
    I am sipping like a fly,—
Like a fly or gnat on Ida   5
    At the hour of goblet-pledge,
By queen Juno brushed aside, a
    Full white arm-sweep, from the edge.

II.

Sooth, the drinking should be ampler
    When the drink is so divine,   10
And some deep-mouthed Greek exemplar
    Would become your Cyprus wine:
Cyclops' mouth might plunge aright in,
    While his one eye overleered,
Nor too large were mouth of Titan   15
    Drinking rivers down his beard.

III.

Pan might dip his head so deep in,
    That his ears alone pricked out,
Fauns around him pressing, leaping,
    Each one pointing to his throat: 20
While the Naiads, like Bacchantes,
    Wild, with urns thrown out to waste,
Cry, 'O earth, that thou wouldst grant us
    Springs to keep, of such a taste!'

IV.

But for me, I am not worthy   25
   After gods and Greeks to drink,
And my lips are pale and earthy
   To go bathing from this brink:
Since you heard them speak the last time,
   They have faded from their blooms,   30
And the laughter of my pastime
   Has learnt silence at the tombs.

V.

Ah, my friend! the antique drinkers
   Crowned the cup and crowned the brow.
Can I answer the old thinkers   35
   In the forms they thought of, now?
Who will fetch from garden-closes
   Some new garlands while I speak,
That the forehead, crowned with roses,
   May strike scarlet down the cheek?   40

VI.

Do not mock me! with my mortal
   Suits no wreath again, indeed;
I am sad-voiced as the turtle
   Which Anacreon used to feed:
Yet as that same bird demurely   45
   Wet her beak in cup of his,
So, without a garland, surely
   I may touch the brim of this.

VII.

Go,—let others praise the Chian!
   This is soft as Muses' string,   50
This is tawny as Rhea's lion,

This is rapid as his spring,
 Bright as Paphia's eyes e'er met us,
  Light as ever trod her feet;
And the brown bees of Hymettus   55
  Make their honey not so sweet.

VIII.

Very copious are my praises,
  Though I sip it like a fly!
Ah—but, sipping,—times and places
  Change before me suddenly: 60
As Ulysses' old libation
  Drew the ghosts from every part,
So your Cyprus wine, dear Grecian,
  Stirs the Hades of my heart.

IX.

And I think of those long mornings   65
  Which my thought goes far to seek,
When, betwixt the folio's turnings,
  Solemn flowed the rhythmic Greek:
Past the pane the mountain spreading,
  Swept the sheep's-bell's tinkling noise,
While a girlish voice was reading,   71
  Somewhat low for *ai*'s and *oi*'s.

X.

Then, what golden hours were for us!
  While we sat together there,
How the white vests of the chorus   75
  Seemed to wave up a live air!
How the cothurns trod majestic
  Down the deep iambic lines,
And the rolling anapæstic
  Curled like vapour over shrines!   80

XI.

Oh, our Æschylus, the thunderous,
    How he drove the bolted breath
Through the cloud to wedge it ponderous
    In the gnarlèd oak beneath!
Oh, our Sophocles, the royal,   85
    Who was born to monarch's place.
And who made the whole world loyal
    Less by kingly power than grace!

XII.

Our Euripides, the human,
    With his droppings of warm tears,   90
And his touches of things common
    Till they rose to touch the spheres!
Our Theocritus, our Bion,
    And our Pindar's shining goals!—
These were cup-bearers undying   95
    Of the wine that's meant for souls.

XIII.

And my Plato, the divine one,
    If men know the gods aright
By their motions as they shine on
    With a glorious trail of light!   100
And your noble Christian bishops,
    Who mouthed grandly the last Greek!
Though the sponges on their hyssops
    Were distent with wine—too weak.

XIV.

Yet, your Chrysostom, you praised him   105
    As a liberal mouth of gold;
And your Basil, you upraised him

75

To the height of speakers old:
And we both praised Heliodorus
   For his secret of pure lies,— 110
Who forged first his linkèd stories
   In the heat of ladies' eyes.

XV.

And we both praised your Synesius
   For the fire shot up his odes,
Though the Church was scarce propitious 115
   As he whistled dogs and gods.
And we both praised Nazianzen
   For the fervid heart and speech:
Only I eschewed his glancing
   At the lyre hung out of reach. 120

XVI.

Do you mind that deed of Atè
   Which you bound me to so fast,—
Reading 'De Virginitate,'
   From the first line to the last?
How I said at ending, solemn 125
   As I turned and looked at you,
That Saint Simeon on the column
   Had had somewhat less to do?

XVII.

For we sometimes gently wrangled,
   Very gently, be it said, 130
Since our thoughts were disentangled
   By no breaking of the thread!
And I charged you with extortions
   On the nobler fames of old—
Ay, and sometimes thought your Porsons 135
   Stained the purple they would fold.

XVIII.

For the rest—a mystic moaning
    Kept Cassandra at the gate,
With wild eyes the vision shone in,
    And wide nostrils scenting fate.   140
And Prometheus, bound in passion
    By brute Force to the blind stone,
Showed us looks of invocation
    Turned to ocean and the sun.

XIX.

And Medea we saw burning   145
    At her nature's planted stake:
And proud Œdipus fate-scorning
    While the cloud came on to break—
While the cloud came on slow, slower,
    Till he stood discrowned, resigned!—   150
But the reader's voice dropped lower
    When the poet called him BLIND.

XX.

Ah, my gossip! you were older,
    And more learned, and a man!
Yet that shadow, the enfolder   155
    Of your quiet eyelids, ran
Both our spirits to one level;
    And I turned from hill and lea
And the summer-sun's green revel,
    To your eyes that could not see.   160

XXI.

Now Christ bless you with the one light
    Which goes shining night and day!
May the flowers which grow in sunlight

Shed their fragrance in your way!
Is it not right to remember   165
    All your kindness, friend of mine,
When we two sat in the chamber,
    And the poets poured us wine?

XXII.

So, to come back to the drinking
    Of this Cyprus,—it is well,   170
But those memories, to my thinking,
    Make a better œnomel;
And whoever be the speaker,
    None can murmur with a sigh
That, in drinking from *that* beaker,   175
    I am sipping like a fly.

THE ROMANCE OF THE SWAN'S NEST

'So the dreams depart,
So the fading phantoms flee,
And the sharp reality
Now must act its part.'   WESTWOOD'S *Beads from a Rosary.*

    I.
Little Ellie sits alone
    'Mid the beeches of a meadow,
        By a stream-side on the grass,
And the trees are showering down
    Doubles of their leaves in shadow   5
        On her shining hair and face.

    II.
She has thrown her bonnet by,
    And her feet she has been dipping

78

In the shallow water's flow:
Now she holds them nakedly   10
   In her hands, all sleek and dripping,
      While she rocketh to and fro.

III.
Little Ellie sits alone,
   And the smile she softly uses
      Fills the silence like a speech,   15
While she thinks what shall be done,
   And the sweetest pleasure chooses
      For her future within reach.

IV.
Little Ellie in her smile
   Chooses—'I will have a lover   20
      Riding on a steed of steeds:
He shall love me without guile,
   And to *him* I will discover
      The swan's nest among the reeds.

V.
'And the steed shall be red-roan,   25
   And the lover shall be noble,
      With an eye that takes the breath:
And the lute he plays upon
   Shall strike ladies into trouble,
      As his sword strikes men to death.   30

VI.
'And the steed it shall be shod
   All in silver, housed in azure.
      And the mane shall swim the wind;
   And the hoofs along the sod

Shall flash onward and keep measure,   35
    Till the shepherds look behind.

VII.
'But my lover will not prize
    All the glory that he rides in,
        When he gazes in my face:
He will say, 'O Love, thine eyes   40
    Build the shrine my soul abides in,
        And I kneel here for thy grace!'

VIII.
'Then, ay, then he shall kneel low,
    With the red-roan steed anear him
        Which shall seem to understand,   45
Till I answer, "Rise and go!
    For the world must love and fear him
        Whom I gift with heart and hand."

IX.
'Then he will arise so pale,
    I shall feel my own lips tremble   50
        With a *yes* I must not say,
Nathless maiden-brave, "Farewell,"
    I will utter, and dissemble—
        "Light to-morrow with to-day!"

X.
'Then he'll ride among the hills   55
    To the wide world past the river,
        There to put away all wrong;
To make straight distorted wills,
    And to empty the broad quiver
        Which the wicked bear along.   60

XI.

'Three times shall a young foot-page
  Swim the stream and climb the mountain
    And kneel down beside my feet—
"Lo, my master sends this gage,
  Lady, for thy pity's counting!   65
    What wilt thou exchange for it?"

XII.

'And the first time I will send
  A white rosebud for a guerdon,
    And the second time, a glove;
But the third time—I may bend   70
  From my pride, and answer—"Pardon
    If he comes to take my love.'

XIII.

'Then the young foot-page will run,
  Then my lover will ride faster,
    Till he kneeleth at my knee: 75
"I am a duke's eldest son,
  Thousand serfs do call me master,
    But, O Love, I love but *thee!*"

XIV.

'He will kiss me on the mouth
  Then, and lead me as a lover   80
    Through the crowds that praise his deeds;
And, when soul-tied by one troth,
  Unto *him* I will discover
    That swan's nest among the reeds.'

XV.

Little Ellie with her smile   85
  Not yet ended, rose up gaily,

Tied the bonnet, donned the shoe,
And went homeward, round a mile,
    Just to see, as she did daily,
        What more eggs were with the two.   90

    XVI.
Pushing through the elm-tree copse,
    Winding up the stream, light-hearted,
        Where the osier pathway leads,
Past the boughs she stoops—and stops.
    Lo, the wild swan had deserted,   95
        And a rat had gnawed the reeds!

    XVII.
Ellie went home sad and slow.
    If she found the lover ever,
        With his red-roan steed of steeds,
Sooth I know not; but I know
    She could never show him—never,
        That swan's nest among the reeds!

[*POEMS* 1850]
HECTOR IN THE GARDEN

    I.
Nine years old! The first of any
    Seem the happiest years that come:
    Yet when *I* was nine, I said
    No such word! I thought instead
That the Greeks had used as many   5
    In besieging Ilium.

    II.
Nine green years had scarcely brought me
    To my childhood's haunted spring;

I had life, like flowers and bees,
  In betwixt the country trees,
And the sun the pleasure taught me
  Which he teacheth every thing.

  III.
If the rain fell, there was sorrow:
  Little head leant on the pane,
  Little finger drawing down it
  The long trailing drops upon it,
And the 'Rain, rain, come to-morrow,'
  Said for charm against the rain.

  IV.
Such a charm was right Canidian,
  Though you meet it with a jeer!
  If I said it long enough,
  Then the rain hummed dimly off,
And the thrush with his pure Lydian
  Was left only to the ear;

  V.
And the sun and I together
  Went a-rushing out of doors:
  We our tender spirits drew
  Over hill and dale in view,
Glimmering hither, glimmering thither
  In the footsteps of the showers.

  VI.
Underneath the chestnuts dripping,
  Through the grasses wet and fair,
  Straight I sought my garden-ground
  With the laurel on the mound,

10

15

20

25

30

And the pear-tree oversweeping   35
    A side-shadow of green air.

   VII.

In the garden lay supinely
    A huge giant wrought of spade!
    Arms and legs were stretched at length
    In a passive giant strength,—   40
The fine meadow turf, cut finely,
    Round them laid and interlaid.

   VIII.

Call him Hector, son of Priam!
    Such his title and degree.
    With my rake I smoothed his brow,   45
    Both his cheeks I weeded through,
But a rhymer such as I am,
    Scarce can sing his dignity.

   IX.

Eyes of gentianellas azure,
    Staring, winking at the skies: 50
    Nose of gillyflowers and box;
    Scented grasses put for locks,
Which a little breeze at pleasure
    Set a-waving round his eyes:

   X.

Brazen helm of daffodillies,   55
    With a glitter toward the light;
    Purple violets for the mouth,
    Breathing perfumes west and south;
And a sword of flashing lilies,
    Holden ready for the fight: 60

XI.

And a breast-plate made of daisies,
   Closely fitting, leaf on leaf;
   Periwinkles interlaced
   Drawn for belt around the waist;
While the brown bees, humming praises,
   Shot their arrows round the chief.   65

XII.

And who knows (I sometimes wondered)
   If the disembodied soul
   Of old Hector, once of Troy,
   Might not take a dreary joy   70
Here to enter—if it thundered,
   Rolling up the thunder-roll?

XIII.

Rolling this way from Troy-ruin,
   In this body rude and rife
   Just to enter, and take rest   75
   'Neath the daisies of the breast—
They, with tender roots, renewing
   His heroic heart to life?

XIV.

Who could know? I sometimes started
   At a motion or a sound!
   Did his mouth speak—naming Troy
   With an *otototototoi*?
Did the pulse of the Strong-hearted
   Make the daisies tremble round?

XV.

It was hard to answer, often: 85
   But the birds sang in the tree.

But the little birds sang bold
  In the pear-tree green and old,
And my terror seemed to soften
  Through the courage of their glee.   90

  XVI.
Oh, the birds, the tree, the ruddy
  And white blossoms sleek with rain!
  Oh, my garden rich with pansies!
  Oh, my childhood's bright romances!
All revive, like Hector's body,   95
  And I see them stir again.

  XVII.
And despite life's changes, chances,
  And despite the deathbell's toll.
  They press on me in full seeming
  Help, some angel! stay this dreaming!   100
As the birds sang in the branches,
 . Sing God's patience through my soul!

  XVIII.
That no dreamer, no neglecter
  Of the present's work unsped,
  I may wake up and be doing,   105
  Life's heroic ends pursuing,
Though my past is dead as Hector,
  And though Hector is twice dead.

MOUNTAINEER AND POET

The simple goatherd between Alp and sky,
Seeing his shadow, in that awful tryst,

Dilated to a giant's on the mist,
Esteems not his own stature larger by
The apparent image, but more patiently
Strikes his staff down beneath his clenching fist,
While the snow-mountains lift their amethyst
And sapphire crowns of splendour, far and nigh,
Into the air around him. Learn from hence
Meek morals, all ye poets that pursue
Your way still onward up to eminence!
Ye are not great because creation drew
Large revelations round your earliest sense,
Nor bright because God's glory shines for you.

A WOMAN'S SHORTCOMINGS

I.

She has laughed as softly as if she sighed,
    She has counted six, and over,
Of a purse well filled and a heart well tried—
    Oh, each a worthy lover!
They 'give her time;' for her soul must slip
    Where the world has set the grooving;
She will lie to none with her fair red lip:
    But love seeks truer loving.

II.

She trembles her fan in a sweetness dumb,
    As her thoughts were beyond recalling,
With a glance for *one*, and a glance for *some*,
    From her eyelids rising and falling;
Speaks common words with a blushful air,
    Hears bold words, unreproving;

But her silence says—what she never will swear—
    And love seeks better loving.

III.

Go, lady, lean to the night-guitar
    And drop a smile to the bringer;
Then smile as sweetly, when he is far,
    At the voice of an in-door singer.
Bask tenderly beneath tender eyes;
    Glance lightly, on their removing;
And join new vows to old perjuries—
    But dare not call it loving.

IV.

Unless you can think, when the song is done,
    No other is soft in the rhythm;
Unless you can feel, when left by One,
    That all men else go with him;
Unless you can know, when unpraised by his breath,
    That your beauty itself wants proving;
Unless you can swear 'For life, for death!'—
    Oh, fear to call it loving!

V.

Unless you can muse in a crowd all day
    On the absent face that fixed you;
Unless you can love, as the angels may,
    With the breadth of heaven betwixt you;
Unless you can dream that his faith is fast,
    Through behoving and unbehoving;
Unless you can *die* when the dream is past—
    Oh, never call it loving!

CHANGE UPON CHANGE

I.

Five months ago the stream did flow,
　　The lilies bloomed within the sedge,
And we were lingering to and fro,
Where none will track thee in this snow,
　　Along the stream beside the hedge.
Ah, Sweet, be free to love and go!
　　For if I do not hear thy foot,
　　The frozen river is as mute,
　　The flowers have dried down to the root:
　　And why, since these be changed since May,
　　　　Shouldst *thou* change less than *they*?

II.

And slow, slow as the winter snow
　　The tears have drifted to mine eyes;
And my poor cheeks, five months ago
Set blushing at thy praises so,
　　Put paleness on for a disguise.
Ah Sweet, be free to praise and go!
　　For if my face is turned too pale,
　　It was thine oath that first did fail,—
　　It was thy love proved false and frail,—
　　And why, since these be changed enow,
　　　　Should *I* change less than *thou*?

SONNETS FROM THE PORTUGUESE (1847-1850)

XIII.

And wilt thou have me fashion into speech
　　The love I bear thee, finding words enough,

89

And hold the torch out, while the winds are rough,
Between our faces, to cast light on each?—
I drop it at thy feet. I cannot teach
My hand to hold my spirit so far off
From myself—me—that I should bring thee proof
In words, of love hid in me out of reach.
Nay, let the silence of my womanhood
Commend my woman-love to thy belief,—
Seeing that I stand unwon, however wooed,
And rend the garment of my life, in brief,
By a most dauntless, voiceless fortitude,
Lest one touch of this heart convey its grief.

XIV.

If thou must love me, let it be for nought
Except for love's sake only. Do not say
'I love her for her smile—her look—her way
Of speaking gently,—for a trick of thought
That falls in well with mine, and certes brought
A sense of pleasant ease on such a day'—
For these things in themselves, Belovèd, may
Be changed, or change for thee,—and love, so wrought,
May be unwrought so. Neither love me for
Thine own dear pity's wiping my cheeks dry,—
A creature might forget to weep, who bore
Thy comfort long, and lose thy love thereby!
But love me for love's sake, that evermore
Thou mayst love on, through love's eternity.

XXIX.

I think of thee!—my thoughts do twine and bud
About thee, as wild vines, about a tree,
Put out broad leaves, and soon there's nought to see
Except the straggling green which hides the wood.

Yet, O my palm-tree, be it understood
I will not have my thoughts instead of thee
Who art dearer, better! Rather, instantly
Renew thy presence; as a strong tree should,
Rustle thy boughs and set thy trunk all bare,
And let these bands of greenery which insphere thee
Drop heavily down,—burst, shattered, everywhere!
Because, in this deep joy to see and hear thee
And breathe within thy shadow a new air,
I do not think of thee—I am too near thee.

XXXVI.

When we met first and loved, I did not build
Upon the event with marble. Could it mean
To last, a love set pendulous between
Sorrow and sorrow? Nay, I rather thrilled,
Distrusting every light that seemed to gild
The onward path, and feared to overlean
A finger even. And, though I have grown serene
And strong since then, I think that God has willed
A still renewable fear . . . O love, O troth . . .
Lest these enclaspèd hands should never hold,
This mutual kiss drop down between us both
As an unowned thing, once the lips being cold.
And Love, be false! if *he*, to keep one oath,
Must lose one joy, by his life's star foretold.

XXXVII.

Pardon, oh, pardon, that my soul should make,
Of all that strong divineness which I know
For thine and thee, an image only so
Formed of the sand, and fit to shift and break.
It is that distant years which did not take
Thy sovranty, recoiling with a blow,

Have forced my swimming brain to undergo
Their doubt and dread, and blindly to forsake
Thy purity of likeness and distort
Thy worthiest love to a worthless counterfeit:
As if a shipwrecked Pagan, safe in port,
His guardian sea-god to commemorate,
Should set a sculptured porpoise, gills a-snort
And vibrant tail, within the temple-gate.

from CASA GUIDI WINDOWS (1851)

A POEM IN TWO PARTS

PART I.

I heard last night a little child go singing
    'Neath Casa Guidi windows, by the church,
O bella libertà, O bella!—stringing
    The same words still on notes he went in search
So high for, you concluded the upspringing   5
    Of such a nimble bird to sky from perch
Must leave the whole bush in a tremble green,
    And that the heat of Italy must beat,
While such a voice had leave to rise serene
    'Twixt church and palace of a Florence street: 10
A little child, too, who not long had been
    By mother's finger steadied on his feet,
And still *O bella libertà* he sang.

Then I thought, musing, of the innumerous
    Sweet songs which still for Italy outrang   15
From older singers' lips who sang not thus
    Exultingly and purely, yet with pang
Fast sheathed in music, touched the heart of us
    So finely that the pity scarcely pained.

I thought how Filicaja led on others,   20
    Bewailers for their Italy enchained,
And how they called her childless among mothers,
    Widow of empires, ay, and scarce refrained
Cursing her beauty to her face, as brothers
    Might a shamed sister's,—'Had she been less fair   25
She were less wretched;'—how, evoking so
    From congregated wrong and heaped despair
Of men and women writhing under blow,
    Harrowed and hideous in a filthy lair,
Some personating Image wherein woe   30
    Was wrapt in beauty from offending much,
They called it Cybele, or Niobe,
    Or laid it corpse-like on a bier for such,
Where all the world might drop for Italy
    Those cadenced tears which burn not where they touch,—   35
'Juliet of nations, canst thou die as we?
    And was the violet crown that crowned thy head
So over-large, though new buds made it rough,
    It slipped down and across thine eyelids dead,
O sweet, fair Juliet?' Of such songs enough,   40
    Too many of such complaints! behold, instead,
Void at Verona, Juliet's marble trough:
    As void as that is, are all images
Men set between themselves and actual wrong,
    To catch the weight of pity, meet the stress   45
Of conscience,—since 'tis easier to gaze long
    On mournful masks and sad effigies
Than on real, live, weak creatures crushed by strong.

[. . .]
I do believe, divinest Angelo,
    That winter-hour in Via Larga, when
They bade thee build a statue up in snow   100

And straight that marvel of thine art again
Dissolved beneath the sun's Italian glow,
   Thine eyes, dilated with the plastic passion,
Thawing too in drops of wounded manhood, since,
   To mock alike thine art and indignation,   105
Laughed at the palace-window the new prince,—
   ('Aha! this genius needs for exaltation,
When all's said and howe'er the proud may wince,
   A little marble from our princely mines!')
I do believe that hour thou laughedst too   110
   For the whole sad world and for thy Florentines,
After those few tears, which were only few!
   That as, beneath the sun, the grand white lines
Of thy snow-statue trembled and withdrew,—
   The head, erect as Jove's, being palsied first,   115
The eyelids flattened, the full brow turned blank,
   The right-hand, raised but now as if it cursed,
Dropt, a mere snowball, (till the people sank
   Their voices, though a louder laughter burst
From the royal window)—thou couldst proudly thank   120
   God and the prince for promise and presage,
And laugh the laugh back, I think verily,
   Thine eyes being purged by tears of righteous rage
To read a wrong into a prophecy,
   And measure a true great man's heritage   125
Against a mere great-duke's posterity.
   I think thy soul said then, 'I do not need
A princedom and its quarries, after all;
   For if I write, paint, carve a word, indeed,
On book or board or dust, on floor or wall,   130
   The same is kept of God who taketh heed
That not a letter of the meaning fall
   Or ere it touch and teach His world's deep heart,
Outlasting, therefore, all your lordships, sir!

So keep your stone, beseech you, for your part, 135
To cover up your grave-place and refer
    The proper titles; *I* live by my art.
The thought I threw into this snow shall stir
    This gazing people when their gaze is done; 140
And the tradition of your act and mine,
    When all the snow is melted in the sun,
Shall gather up, for unborn men, a sign
    Of what is the true princedom,—ay, and none
Shall laugh that day, except the drunk with wine.'
[. . .]

PART II.
[. . .]
    From Casa Guidi windows I looked out, 100
Again looked and beheld a different sight.
    The Duke had fled before the people's shout
'Long live the Duke!' A people, to speak right,
    Must speak as soft as courtiers, lest a doubt
Should curdle brows of gracious sovereigns, white. 105
    Moreover that same dangerous shouting meant
Some gratitude for future favours, which
    Were only promised, the Constituent
Implied, the whole being subject to the hitch
    In 'motu proprios,' very incident 110
To all these Czars, from Paul to Paulovitch.
    Whereat the people rose up in the dust
Of the ruler's flying feet, and shouted still
    And loudly; only, this time, as was just,
Not 'Live the Duke,' who had fled for good or ill, 115
    But 'Live the People,' who remained and must,
The unrenounced and unrenounceable.
    Long live the people! How they lived! and boiled
And bubbled in the cauldron of the street:

How the young blustered, nor the old recoiled,   120
And what a thunderous stir of tongues and feet
    Trod flat the palpitating bells and foiled
The joy-guns of their echo, shattering it!
    How down they pulled the Duke's arms everywhere!
How up they set new café-signs, to show   125
    Where patriots might sip ices in pure air—
(The fresh paint smelling somewhat)! To and fro
    How marched the civil guard, and stopped to stare
When boys broke windows in a civic glow!
    How rebel songs were sung to loyal tunes,   130
And bishops cursed in ecclesiastic metres:
    How all the Circoli grew large as moons,
And all the speakers, moonstruck,—thankful greeters
    Of prospects which struck poor the ducal boons,
A mere free Press, and Chambers!—frank repeaters   135
    Of great Guerazzi's praises—'There's a man,
The father of the land, who, truly great,
    Takes off that national disgrace and ban,
The farthing tax upon our Florence-gate,
    And saves Italia as he only can!'   140
How all the nobles fled, and would not wait,
    Because they were most noble,—which being so,
How Liberals vowed to burn their palaces,
    Because free Tuscans were not free to go!
How grown men raged at Austria's wickedness,   145
    And smoked,—while fifty striplings in a row
Marched straight to Piedmont for the wrong's redress!
    You say we failed in duty, we who wore
Black velvet like Italian democrats,
    Who slashed our sleeves like patriots, nor forswore   150
The true republic in the form of hats?
    We chased the archbishop from the Duomo door,
We chalked the walls with bloody caveats

Against all tyrants. If we did not fight
Exactly, we fired muskets up the air   155
    To show that victory was ours of right.
We met, had free discussion everywhere
    (Except perhaps i' the Chambers) day and night.
We proved the poor should be employed, . . . that's fair,—
    And yet the rich not worked for anywise,—   160
Pay certified, yet payers abrogated,—
    Full work secured, yet liabilities
To overwork excluded,—not one bated
    Of all our holidays, that still, at twice
Or thrice a week, are moderately rated.   165
    We proved that Austria was dislodged, or would
Or should be, and that Tuscany in arms
    Should, would dislodge her, ending the old feud;
And yet, to leave our piazzas, shops, and farms,
    For the simple sake of fighting, was not good—   170
We proved that also. 'Did we carry charms
    Against being killed ourselves, that we should rush
On killing others? what, desert herewith
    Our wives and mothers?—was that duty? tush!'
At which we shook the sword within the sheath   175
    Like heroes—only louder; and the flush
Ran up the cheek to meet the future wreath.
    Nay, what we proved, we shouted—how we shouted
(Especially the boys did), boldly planting
    That tree of liberty, whose fruit is doubted,   180
Because the roots are not of nature's granting!
    A tree of good and evil: none, without it,
Grow gods; alas and, with it, men are wanting!
[. . .]

from AURORA LEIGH (1856)

A POEM IN NINE BOOKS

At this point in the narrative Aurora, staying with her aunt and occupied with domestic pastime, meets her cousin Romney Leigh. He, a wealthy yet philanthropically inclined young man, and she, with an ardent poetic nature, engage in discussion. He is not un-attractive to her, and he proposes. This has the effect of sending her off to study and to think in London because, at this stage, she realizes their incompatibility.

BOOK II.

[. . .]

'There it is!—
You play beside a death-bed like a child,   180
Yet measure to yourself a prophet's place
To teach the living. None of all these things
Can women understand. You generalise
Oh, nothing,—not even grief! Your quick-breathed hearts,
So sympathetic to the personal pang,   185
Close on each separate knife-stroke, yielding up
A whole life at each wound, incapable
Of deepening, widening a large lap of life
To hold the world-full woe. The human race
To you means, such a child, or such a man,   190
You saw one morning waiting in the cold,
Beside that gate, perhaps. You gather up
A few such cases, and when strong sometimes
Will write of factories and of slaves, as if
Your father were a negro, and your son   195
A spinner in the mills. All's yours and you,
All, coloured with your blood, or otherwise
Just nothing to you. Why, I call you hard
To general suffering. Here's the world half-blind

With intellectual light, half-brutalised 200
With civilisation, having caught the plague
In silks from Tarsus, shrieking east and west
Along a thousand railroads, mad with pain
And sin too! . . . does one woman of you all
(You who weep easily) grow pale to see 205
This tiger shake his cage?—does one of you
Stand still from dancing, stop from stringing pearls,
And pine and die because of the great sum
Of universal anguish?—Show me a tear
Wet as Cordelia's, in eyes bright as yours, 210
Because the world is mad. You cannot count,
That you should weep for this account, not you!
You weep for what you know. A red-haired child
Sick in a fever, if you touch him once,
Though but so little as with a finger-tip, 215
Will set you weeping; but a million sick . . .
You could as soon weep for the rule of three
Or compound fractions. Therefore, this same world,
Uncomprehended by you, must remain
Uninfluenced by you.—Women as you are, 220
Mere women, personal and passionate,
You give us doating mothers, and perfect wives,
Sublime Madonnas, and enduring saints!
We get no Christ from you,—and verily
We shall not get a poet, in my mind.' 225
'With which conclusion you conclude' . . .
                                          'But this,'
That you, Aurora, with the large live brow
And steady eyelids, cannot condescend
To play at art, as children play at swords,
To show a pretty spirit, chiefly admired 230
Because true action is impossible.
You never can be satisfied with praise

99

Which men give women when they judge a book
Not as mere work but as mere woman's work,
Expressing the comparative respect   235
Which means the absolute scorn. 'Oh, excellent.
'What grace, what facile turns, what fluent sweeps,
'What delicate discernment . . . almost thought!
'The book does honour to the sex, we hold.
'Among our female authors we make room   240
'For this fair writer, and congratulate
'The country that produces in these times
'Such women, competent to . . . spell.'
                                        'Stop there,'
I answered, burning through his thread of talk
With a quick flame of emotion,—'You have read   245
My soul, if not my book, and argue well
I would not condescend . . . we will not say
To such a kind of praise (a worthless end
Is praise of all kinds), but to such a use
Of holy art and golden life. I am young,   250
And peradventure weak—you tell me so—
Through being a woman. And, for all the rest,
Take thanks for justice. I would rather dance
At fairs on tight-rope, till the babies dropped
Their gingerbread for joy,—than shift the types   255
For tolerable verse, intolerable
To men who act and suffer. Better far
Pursue a frivolous trade by serious means,
Than a sublime art frivolously.'
[. . .]

AN AUGUST VOICE (*POEMS BEFORE CONGRESS* 1860)

'Una voce augusta.'—MONITORE TOSCANO

I.

You'll take back your Grand-duke?
   I made the treaty upon it.
Just venture a quiet rebuke;
   Dall' Ongaro write him a sonnet;
Ricasoli gently explain   5
   Some need of the constitution:
He'll swear to it over again,
   Providing an 'easy solution.'
You'll call back the Grand-duke.

II.

You'll take back your Grand-duke?   10
   I promised the Emperor Francis
To argue the case by his book,
   And ask you to meet his advances.
The Ducal cause, we know
   (Whether you or he be the wronger),   15
Has very strong points;—although
   Your bayonets, there, have stronger.
You'll call back the Grand-duke.

III.

You'll take back your Grand-duke?
   He is not pure altogether.   20
For instance, the oath which he took
   (In the Forty-eight rough weather)
He'd 'nail your flag to his mast,'
   Then softly scuttled the boat you
Hoped to escape in at last,   25
   And both by a 'Proprio motu.'
You'll call back the Grand-duke.

IV.

You'll take back your Grand-duke?
    The scheme meets nothing to shock it
In this smart letter, look, 30
    We found in Radetsky's pocket;
Where his Highness in sprightly style
    Of the flower of his Tuscans wrote,
'These heads be the hottest in file;
    Pray shoot them the quickest.' Quote. 35
And call back the Grand-duke.

V.

You'll take back your Grand-duke?
    There *are* some things to object to.
He cheated, betrayed, and forsook,
    Then called in the foe to protect you. 40
He taxed you for wines and for meats
    Throughout that eight years' pastime
Of Austria's drum in your streets—
    Of course you remember the last time
You called back your Grand-duke? 45

VI.

You'll take back the Grand-duke?
    It is not race he is poor in,
Although he never could brook
    The patriot cousin at Turin.
His love of kin you discern, 50
    By his hate of your flag and me—
So decidedly apt to turn
    All colours at the sight of the Three.
You'll call back the Grand-duke.

VII.

You'll take back your Grand-duke?   55
    'Twas weak that he fled from the Pitti;
But consider how little he shook
    At thought of bombarding your city!
And, balancing that with this,
    The Christian rule is plain for us;   60
. . . Or the Holy Father's Swiss
    Have shot his Perugians in vain for us.
You'll call back the Grand-duke.

VIII.

Pray take back your Grand-duke.
    —I, too, have suffered persuasion.   65
All Europe, raven and rook,
    Screeched at me armed for your nation.
Your cause in my heart struck spurs;
    I swept such warnings aside for you:
My very child's eyes, and Hers,   70
    Grew like my brother's who died for you.
You'll call back the Grand-duke?

IX.

You'll take back your Grand-duke?
    My French fought nobly with reason,—
Left many a Lombardy nook   75
    Red as with wine out of season.
Little we grudged what was done there,
    Paid freely your ransom of blood:
Our heroes stark in the sun there
    We would not recall if we could.   80
You'll call back the Grand-duke?

103

X.

You'll take back your Grand-duke?
   His son rode fast as he got off
That day on the enemy's hook,
   When *I* had an epaulette shot off.   85
Though splashed (as I saw him afar—no,
   Near) by those ghastly rains,
The mark, when you've washed him in Arno,
   Will scarcely be larger than Cain's.
You'll call back the Grand-duke?   90

XI.

You'll take back your Grand-duke?
   'Twill be so simple, quite beautiful:
The shepherd recovers his crook,
   . . . If you should be sheep, and dutiful.
I spoke a word worth chalking   95
   On Milan's wall—but stay,
Here's Poniatowsky talking,—
   You'll listen to *him* to-day,
And call back the Grand-duke.

XII.

You'll take back your Grand-duke?   100
   Observe, there's no one to force it,—
Unless the Madonna, Saint Luke
   Drew for you, choose to endorse it.
I charge you, by great Saint Martino
   And prodigies quickened by wrong,   105
Remember your Dead on Ticino;
   Be worthy, be constant, be strong—
Bah!—call back the Grand-duke!!

LORD WALTER'S WIFE

I.
'But why do you go?' said the lady, while both sat under the yew,
And her eyes were alive in their depth, as the kraken beneath the
    sea-blue.

II.
'Because I fear you,' he answered;—'because you are far too fair,
And able to strangle my soul in a mesh of your gold-coloured hair.'

III.
'Oh, that,' she said, 'is no reason! Such knots are quickly undone,   5
And too much beauty, I reckon, is nothing but too much sun.'

IV.
'Yet farewell so,' he answered;—'the sun-stroke's fatal at times.
I value your husband, Lord Walter, whose gallop rings still from
    the limes.'

V.
'Oh, that,' she said, 'is no reason. You smell a rose through a fence.
If two should smell it, what matter? who grumbles, and where's
    the pretence?'   10

VI.
'But I,' he replied, 'have promised another, when love was free,
To love her alone, alone, who alone and afar loves me.'

VII.
'Why, that,' she said, 'is no reason, Love's always free, I am told.
Will you vow to be safe from the headache on Tuesday, and think it
    will hold?'

VIII.

'But you,' he replied, 'have a daughter, a young little child, who
    was laid   15
In your lap to be pure: so I leave you: the angels would make me
    afraid.'

IX.

'Oh, that,' she said, 'is no reason. The angels keep out of the way;
And Dora, the child, observes nothing, although you should please
    me and stay.'

X.

At which he rose up in his anger,—'Why, now, you no longer are fair!
Why, now, you no longer are fatal, but ugly and hateful, I swear.' 20

XI.

At which she laughed out in her scorn: 'These men! Oh, these men
    overnice,
Who are shocked if a colour not virtuous is frankly put on by a vice.'

XII.

Her eyes blazed upon him—'And *you*! You bring us your vices
    so near
That we smell them! You think in our presence a thought 'twould
    defame us to hear!

XIII.

'What reason had you, and what right,—I appeal to your soul from
    my life,—   25
To find me too fair as a woman? Why, sir, I am pure, and a wife.

XIV.

'Is the day-star too fair up above you? It burns you not. Dare you imply
I brushed you more close than the star does, when Walter had set me
    as high?

106

XV.

'If a man finds a woman too fair, he means simply adapted too much
To uses unlawful and fatal. The praise!—shall I thank you for such?   30

XVI.

'Too fair?—not unless you misuse us! and surely if, once in a while,
You attain to it, straightway you call us no longer too fair, but too vile.

XVII.

'A moment,—I pray your attention!—I have a poor word in my head
I must utter, though womanly custom would set it down better
    unsaid.

XVIII.

'You grew, sir, pale to impertinence, once when I showed you a
    ring.   35
You kissed my fan when I dropped it. No matter!—I've broken the
    thing.

XIX.

'You did me the honour, perhaps, to be moved at my side now and
    then
In the senses—a vice, I have heard, which is common to beasts and
    some men.

XX.

'Love's a virtue for heroes!—as white as the snow on high hills,
And immortal as every great soul is that struggles, endures, and
    fulfils.   40

XXI.

'I love my Walter profoundly,—you, Maude, though you faltered a
    week,
For the sake of . . . what was it—an eye-brow? or, less still, a mole
    on a cheek?

XXII.

'And since, when all's said, you're too noble to stoop to the frivolous cant

About crimes irresistible, virtues that swindle, betray and supplant,

XXIII.

'I determined to prove to yourself that, whate'er you might dream or avow   45

By illusion, you wanted precisely no more of me than you have now.

XXIV.

'There! Look me full in the face!—in the face. Understand, if you can,

That the eyes of such women as I am are clean as the palm of a man.

XXV.

'Drop his hand, you insult him. Avoid us for fear we should cost you a scar—

You take us for harlots, I tell you, and not for the women we are. 50

XXVI.

'You wronged me: but then I considered . . . there's Walter! And so at the end

I vowed that he should not be mulcted, by me, in the hand of a friend.

XXVII.

'Have I hurt you indeed? We are quits then. Nay, friend of my Walter, be mine!

Come, Dora, my darling, my angel, and help me to ask him to dine.'

BIANCA AMONG THE NIGHTINGALES

I.

The cypress stood up like a church
    That night we felt our love would hold,
And saintly moonlight seemed to search
    And wash the whole world clean as gold;
The olives crystallised the vales'   5
    Broad slopes until the hills grew strong:
The fire-flies and the nightingales
    Throbbed each to either, flame and song.
The nightingales, the nightingales!

II.

Upon the angle of its shade   10
    The cypress stood, self-balanced high;
Half up, half down, as double-made,
    Along the ground, against the sky;
And *we*, too! from such soul-height went
    Such leaps of blood, so blindly driven,   15
We scarce knew if our nature meant
    Most passionate earth or intense heaven.
The nightingales, the nightingales!

III.

We paled with love, we shook with love,
    We kissed so close we could not vow;   20
Till Giulio whispered 'Sweet, above
    God's Ever guaranties this Now.'
And through his words the nightingales
    Drove straight and full their long clear call,
Like arrows through heroic mails,   25
    And love was awful in it all.
The nightingales, the nightingales!

IV.

O cold white moonlight of the north,
    Refresh these pulses, quench this hell!
O coverture of death drawn forth   30
    Across this garden-chamber . . . well!
But what have nightingales to do
    In gloomy England, called the free . . .
(Yes, free to die in! . . .) when we two
    Are sundered, singing still to me?   35
And still they sing, the nightingales!

V.

I think I hear him, how he cried
    'My own soul's life!' between their notes.
Each man has but one soul supplied,
    And that's immortal. Though his throat's   40
On fire with passion now, to her
    He can't say what to me he said!
And yet he moves her, they aver.
    The nightingales sing, through my head,—
The nightingales, the nightingales!   45

VI.

He says to her what moves her most.
    He would not name his soul within
Her hearing,—rather pays her cost
    With praises to her lips and chin.
Man has but one soul, 'tis ordained,   50
    And each soul but one love, I add;
Yet souls are damned and love's profaned;
    These nightingales will sing me mad!
The nightingales, the nightingales!

VII.

I marvel how the birds can sing. 55
    There's little difference, in their view,
Betwixt our Tuscan trees that spring
    As vital flames into the blue,
And dull round blots of foliage meant,
    Like saturated sponges here 60
To suck the fogs up. As content
    Is he too in this land, 'tis clear.
And still they sing, the nightingales.

VIII.

My native Florence! dear, forgone!
    I see across the Alpine ridge 65
How the last feast-day of Saint John
    Shot rockets from Carraia bridge.
The luminous city, tall with fire,
    Trod deep down in that river of ours,
While many a boat with lamp and choir 70
    Skimmed birdlike over glittering towers.
I will not hear these nightingales.

IX.

I seem to float, *we* seem to float
    Down Arno's stream in festive guise;
A boat strikes flame into our boat, 75
    And up that lady seems to rise
As then she rose. The shock had flashed
    A vision on us! What a head,
What leaping eyeballs!—beauty dashed
    To splendour by a sudden dread. 80
And still they sing, the nightingales.

X.

Too bold to sin, too weak to die;
   Such women are so. As for me,
I would we had drowned there, he and I,
   That moment, loving perfectly.   85
He had not caught her with her loosed
   Gold ringlets . . . rarer in the south . . .
Nor heard the 'Grazie tanto' bruised
   To sweetness by her English mouth.
And still they sing, the nightingales.   90

XI.

She had not reached him at my heart
   With her fine tongue, as snakes indeed
Kill flies; nor had I, for my part,
   Yearned after, in my desperate need,
And followed him as he did her   95
   To coasts left bitter by the tide,
Whose very nightingales elsewhere
   Delighting, torture and deride!
For still they sing, the nightingales.

XII.

A worthless woman; mere cold clay   100
   As all false things are: but so fair,
She takes the breath of men away
   Who gaze upon her unaware.
I would not play her larcenous tricks
   To have her looks! She lied and stole,   105
And spat into my love's pure pyx
   The rank saliva of her soul.
And still they sing, the nightingales.

XIII.

I would not for her white and pink,
    Though such he likes—her grace of limb, 110
Though such he has praised—nor yet, I think,
    For life itself, though spent with him,
Commit such sacrilege, affront
    God's nature which is love, intrude
'Twixt two affianced souls, and hunt 115
    Like spiders, in the altar's wood.
I cannot bear these nightingales.

XIV.

If she chose sin, some gentler guise
    She might have sinned in, so it seems:
She might have pricked out both my eyes, 120
    And I still seen him in my dreams!
—Or drugged me in my soup or wine,
    Nor left me angry afterward:
To die here with his hand in mine,
    His breath upon me, were not hard. 125
(Our Lady hush these nightingales!)

XV.

But set a springe for *him*, 'mio ben,'
    My only good, my first last love!—
Though Christ knows well what sin is, when
    He sees some things done they must move 130
Himself to wonder. Let her pass.
    I think of her by night and day.
Must *I* too join her . . . out, alas! . . .
    With Giulio, in each word I say?
And evermore the nightingales! 135

XVI.

Giulio, my Giulio!—sing they so,
    And you be silent? Do I speak,
And you now hear? An arm you throw
    Round some one, and I feel so weak?
—Oh, owl-like birds! They sing for spite,   140
    They sing for hate, they sing for doom,
They'll sing through death who sing through night,
    They'll sing and stun me in the tomb—
The nightingales, the nightingales!

AMY'S CRUELTY

I.

Fair Amy of the terraced house,
    Assist me to discover
Why you who would not hurt a mouse
    Can torture so your lover.

II.

You give your coffee to the cat,   5
    You stroke the dog for coming,
And all your face grows kinder at
    The little brown bee's humming.

III.

But when *he* haunts your door . . . the town
    Marks coming and marks going . . .   10
You seem to have stitched your eyelids down
    To that long piece of sewing!

IV.

You never give a look, not you,
　　Nor drop him a 'Good morning,'
To keep his long day warm and blue,　　　　　　　　15
　　So fretted by your scorning.

V.

She shook her head—'The mouse and bee
　　For crumb or flower will linger:
The dog is happy at my knee,
　　The cat purrs at my finger.　　　　　　　　　　20

VI.

'But *he* . . . to *him*, the least thing given
　　Means great things at a distance;
He wants my world, my sun, my heaven,
　　Soul body, whole existence.

VII.

'They say love gives as well as takes;　　　　　　　25
　　But I'm a simple maiden,—
My mother's first smile when she wakes
　　I still have smiled and prayed in.

VIII.

'I only know my mother's love
　　Which gives all and asks nothing;　　　　　　　30
And this new loving sets the groove
　　Too much the way of loathing.

IX.

'Unless he gives me all in change,
　　I forfeit all things by him:
The risk is terrible and strange—　　　　　　　　35
　　I tremble, doubt, . . . deny him.

X.

'He's sweetest friend or hardest foe,
    Best angel or worst devil;
I either hate or . . . love him so,
    I can't be merely civil!   40

XI.

'You trust a woman who puts forth
    Her blossoms thick as summer's?
You think she dreams what love is worth,
    Who casts it to new-comers?

XII.

'Such love's a cowslip-ball to fling,   45
    A moment's pretty pastime;
I give . . . all me, if anything,
    The first time and the last time.

XIII.

'Dear neighbour of the trellised house,
    A man should murmur never,   50
Though treated worse than dog and mouse,
    Till doated on for ever!'

NOTES TO THE TEXT

BATTLE OF MARATHON: Athenian victory which repulsed the first Persian invasion of Greece (490 B.C.). The whole panoply of the Battle within the context of the Wars is dramatized in Aeschylus's play, *Persians* 472 B.C.).

THE ESSAY ON MIND: ll. 1081-83, in Greek mythology Amphion was given a lyre by the god Hermes, son of Maia, and became a wonderful musician. With his brother Zethus he walled Thebes, 'Boeotia's city', drawing the stones after him by the magical music of his instrument.

LADY GERALDINE'S COURTSHIP: l. 162, William Howitt (1792-1879) miscellaneous writer and poet. Like E. B. B., with his wife he became interested in spiritualism contributing more than one hundred articles on personal experiences to the *Spiritualist Magazine*. l. 227, Luís (Vaz) de Camoëns (1524-1580), great Portuguese poet, author of lyrics, etc., and finest national epic of the Renaissance, *Os Lusiádas* (*The Lusiads*). See E. B. B.'s poem in the text, *Catarina to Camoëns*, alluded to here. l.268, originally the Pythian Games consisted of musicians' contests held in honour of Apollo to celebrate his victory over Python. l. 367, 'Phemius' is the abbreviated name of Polyphemus, the Cyclops.

THE LOST BOWER: William (Robert?) Langland (1330?-1400?), author of *The Vision concerning Piers the Plowman*. The Malvern Hills are the scene of Langland's visions. l. 68, *Rinaldo* is a chivalric poem by the Italian Torquato Tasso (1544-1595). l. 238, 'lusus' = *lusus naturae*, a freak of nature.

CATARINA TO CAMOENS: see note to l. 227, *Lady Geraldine's Courtship*.

WINE OF CYPRUS: l. 49, Chios is a large island lying off the Erythrean peninsula and claims to be the birthplace of Homer. l. 51, Rhea was an ancient Greek goddess of the earth, mistress of wild nature, to whom the lion was sacred. l.53, Paphos was a city near the coast of Cyprus containing a famous temple of Aphrodite, who was believed to have risen from the sea nearby. l. 55, Mount Hymettus, east of Athens, where beekeeping had been practised since antiquity. l. 121, Até was daughter of Zeus, the personification of infatuation (or moral blindness). l. 123, the writings of the early Fathers on virginity are numerous. E. B. B. is probably referring to the *De Virginitate* of St Basil of Ancyra, mentioned in l. 107. l.128, Saint Simeon Stylites (?390-459), first known Christian monk who, apart from occasional acts of charity, was celebrated for practising an extreme form of asceticism, dwelling atop a column until he died. See Tennyson's satirical monologue on the subject. l. 135, Richard Porson (1759-1808), brilliant classical scholar, Professor of Greek at Cambridge, devoted to liberating Greek texts from corruptions.

HECTOR IN THE GARDEN. l. 19, Canidia was a sorceress, often mentioned by the Latin Horace. l 82, *otototototoi*: an exclamation of pain and grief.

CASA GUIDI WINDOWS: Following the (general) revolutions of 1848 Leopold II of Florence, together with other Italian rulers, was compelled to grant a more liberal constitution. In the thrust towards nationalism he sent troops to help challenge the Austrians; but, like the Pope, hastily withdrew them when reverses began. Finding that the democrats were bent on an Italian Constituent Assembly he fled to Gaeta (Feb. 1849). At Florence a predominantly democratic provisional government was formed, but further Austrian victories made the position of the democrats throughout Italy impossible. The Grand Duke Leopold was recalled by the moderates, and he returned with Austrian troops, crushing a democratic insurrection at Livorno (May 1849). Book I, l. 20, Vincenzo da Filicaia (1642-1707), Florentine lyric poet whose sonnets predicted Italian unification; admired by Byron. Book II, l. 3, see note to l. 22, *An August Voice*. l.110, a *motu Proprio* is a Papal document in which the Pope, with all his powers, acts of his own accord. In 1848 Pio Nono published one which appeared to give his blessing to the idea of a united Italy. l. 132, 'Circoli' were revolutionary political clubs. l. 136, Francesco Domenico Guerazzi was a leader of the democrats, whose success caused Leopold to flee to Gaeta. l. 111, a satirical jibe at the progressively degenerate stature of all leaders and their politicizing.

AN AUGUST VOICE: The poem is supposedly spoken by Napoleon III of France who had engaged himself and his troops to fight on the side of the Italians with a view to expelling the Austrians from Italy when the Second War of Independence broke out in 1859. Though he wanted to prevent Italian unity at all costs, he was politically outmanoeuvred by Count Cavour and it looked like becoming a certainty. Leopold II, for example, had fled Florence once more (see note to *Casa Guidi Windows*) and government passed to the moderates. Napoleon, therefore, concluded the Armistice of Villafranca with the Austrian Emperor, Francis Joseph, where, among other matters the restoration of Leopold was arranged. (It is to be noted how E. B. B., a staunch admirer of Napoleon, seems to fail to appreciate his questionable part in the process). The title and epigraph of the poem allude to the terms of the (July) Armistice and play satirically upon the double meaning of 'August/augusta'. A complete edition of the Tuscan *Monitore* was burnt by an incensed mob. l. 4, Francesco Dall' Ongaro was a popular poet and apparent supporter of liberty. l. 5, Baron Bettino Ricasoli emerged as leader of the moderates. l. 22, refers to the conflicts of 1848 and Leopold's flight (July 1849) to Gaeta. l. 31, Marshal Joseph Radetsky (1766-1858) had been the redoubtable commander of the Austrian forces in Italy. l. 56, the Palazzo Pitti was the royal residence, the most imposing of the Florentine palaces. l. 97, Jozef Poniatowski (1816-1873), member of the Tuscan parliament, foreign ambassador, retired (1853) and became a French citizen.